If Bees Are Few

Proceeds from the sale
of *If Bees Are Few: A Hive
of Bee Poems* will be donated
to the Bee Lab in the
Department of Entomology at
the University of Minnesota.
Headed by Dr. Marla Spivak,
MacArthur Fellow and
Distinguished McKnight
Professor in Entomology,
the Bee Lab's research and
educational outreach promote
the health of bee pollinators,
discovering solutions to
protect bees worldwide.

To learn more about the
Bee Lab's groundbreaking
work and resources, and for
more information about how
to support its efforts and
contribute to the health of
bees everywhere, please visit
www.beelab.umn.edu.

If Bees Are Few

A HIVE OF BEE POEMS

JAMES P. LENFESTEY, EDITOR

———— •◦• ————

Foreword by Bill McKibben

Afterword by Marla Spivak

UNIVERSITY OF MINNESOTA PRESS

MINNEAPOLIS • LONDON

The University of Minnesota Press gratefully acknowledges
the generous assistance provided for the publication of
this book by the Margaret W. Harmon Fund.

For copyright and permission information for previously
published material in this book, see pages 221–25.

Published by the University of Minnesota Press
111 Third Avenue South, Suite 290
Minneapolis, MN 55401-2520
http://www.upress.umn.edu

A Cataloging-in-Publication record for this book is available
from the Library of Congress.

ISBN 978-0-8166-9806-6 (hc)
ISBN 978-0-8166-9808-0 (pb)

Printed in the United States of America on acid-free paper

The University of Minnesota is an equal-opportunity
educator and employer.

22 21 20 19 18 17 16   10 9 8 7 6 5 4 3 2 1

Dedicated to Dr. Marla Spivak
and all the entomologists and beekeepers
who study not only honeybees
but also the ecosystems and husbandry they require.
Without them, honeybees have little chance;
with them, they and we have some sweet hope.

Next I'll speak about the celestial gift of honey from the air.

 —Virgil

we pollinate the fields
because we are the fields

 —Nick Flynn

Forget not bees in winter, though they sleep.

 —Victoria Sackville-West

Hurry now, for the hive is ill . . .

 —Brenda Hillman

Contents

Bill McKibben

The bee strikes me as—among other things—a buzzing, hovering metaphor. For so many things.

There's busyness, yes. To lie by the entrance to a hive and watch the endless parade of bees returning, crisply, with their saddlebags of pollen is to understand something about the nature of work. Done steadily, it adds up. A nice conservative truism!

And of course there's the community of the hive. Bees absolutely understand that they are part of something larger than themselves, that they're less individuals than extensions of each other. How progressive is that!

Then there's the royalist queen, controlling all from her throne. But then there's the very democratic process of finding a new home when you swarm—what Tom Seeley in his epic account *Honeybee Democracy* compared to a New England town meeting. There are messages about the sweetness of honey and the pain of the sting, about the short and fervent summer and the long torpid winter. You'll find, I think, these images abounding in this remarkable collection of tributes to the humble, astonishing bee.

But two ideas I want to highlight here at the start sometimes seem to me less prominent when we consider these other communities. One is the role bees now play as sentinels in an increasingly toxic world. You can think of bees as a kind of early warning system: they head out many times a day to scour the surrounding landscape, leaf by petal, then bring back the news concentrated in nectar. And that news is . . . bad: for the past few years we have seen rapid and large-scale die-offs, which are sending us signals. Those signals are about new chemicals, about new weather, about new patterns of habitation. They are potent warnings that we are out of balance as a society and need to get back in. We ignore them at our peril.

The bees also provide a beautiful example of how we might live in slightly different ways that work better for us and the world. They have allowed the beekeeper to establish a fairly remarkable relationship, unlike almost any other we know. Honeybees clearly remain wild animals, out in the world beyond fence or pen. Yet they return to the hive, where the wise beekeeper takes a little of their surplus but promises to lavish them with the care they need to get through the hard parts of their year. This is a lovely give-and-take, easily upset by greed or carelessness, but in its constant operation a good reminder that "sufficiency" can be among the finest words in our language.

Language is employed to great good effect in these verses. They are best read, I imagine, while lying in a bee yard on an August afternoon as the bees do their work in the clover fields and the honey crop begins to swell in the supers. May these words bless you almost as much as the calm and constant hum of the hive itself!

James P. Lenfestey

It is said there are twenty thousand species of bees in the world, a genus fifty million years old, but in the fertile imagination of the world's poets, there is no beginning and no end to bee buzz. As Rilke wrote, poets are "bees of the invisible. We wildly collect the honey of the visible, to store it in the great golden hive of the invisible."

Sappho wrote of bees in the sixth century BCE ("neither honey nor bees for me"), as did Virgil, Rumi, Shakespeare, Bobby Burns, Clare, Coleridge, Robert Devereux, second Earl of Essex, Emerson, Herrick, Issa, Machado, Mandelstam, Neruda, Dickinson prolifically, Whitman, Whittier, Tennyson, Yeats, Frost, and on into the distracting buzz of the twentieth and twenty-first centuries, from Sherman Alexie to Timothy Young.

Sylvia Plath's father kept bees, and while living in England she tried it, too. She got six jars of honey and the famous "bee sequence" of poems from 1962, later published in *Ariel*, which convinced her she was a real poet.

During the early seventies, when I ran an experiment in rural education, I kept bees. This fact relates me to Sylvia Plath, whose fortunate gift for language and unfortunate gift for self-destruction I do not possess. But encounters with bees, whether in the guise of a bee-masked holy father or the mysterious swarms themselves, were indeed unforgettable to us both and worthy of praise in poems, if one can only figure out how.

I finally figured out how, and it is this anthology (the word, from ancient Greek, means literally a "gathering of flowers"). *If Bees Are Few* is a gathering of poems collected over the past decade that touch on, or are touched by, bees, including "To make a prairie" by Emily Dickinson:

To make a prairie it takes a clover and one bee.
One clover, and a bee.
And revery.
The revery alone will do
If bees are few.

That poem gives this collection its title, and reverie about bees is what made the bee poems on the following pages. Emily herself wrote more poems touching on bees than almost any other creature in the poetry ecosystem, as if they were "bee guides" into the domestic wildness of her poetic life. Her first three known poems, according to Thomas J. Johnson's chronology, all hold bee references, including this lovely couplet from her very first, sent for Valentine's Week of 1850, when she was nineteen:

The bee doth court the flower, the flower his suit
    receives,
And they make a merry wedding, whose guests
    are hundred leaves.

We are all leaves at that wedding, including the more than one hundred other poets whose honeyed and stinging words are captured here.

THE BEE POETS

On April 15, 1862, Emily Dickinson sent four poems to critic Thomas Wentworth Higginson, asking him whether her poems "breathed. " One of the poems she chose for that introduction used her fondness for bees as a way to illustrate spiritual discovery:

The nearest Dream recedes—unrealized—
The Heaven we chase,
Like the June Bee—before the School Boy,
Invites the Race—
Stoops to an easy Clover—
Dips—evades—teases—deploys—
Then—to the Royal Clouds

Lifts his light Pinnace—
Heedless of the Boy—
Staring—bewildered—at the mocking sky—
Homesick for steadfast Honey—
Ah the Bee flies not
That brews that rare variety!

After a mystified Higginson responded to her (his letter is lost), the elusive Miss Dickinson wrote him again, enclosing four more poems, including another in which the observed behavior of bumblebees opens a Zen-like puzzle of negative space, the central thing "presented here" never named:

South Winds jostle them
Bumblebees come
Hover hesitate
Drink, and are gone

Butterflies pause
On their passage Cashmere
I softly plucking,
Present them here!

Emily knew intimately the throb of nature bees create and define, and the bee/flower rub remained a lifelong transport that she hived in at least twenty-six separate poems.

Yeats's "The Lake Isle of Innisfree" begins with a quatrain:

I will arise and go now, and go to Innisfree,
A small cabin build there of clay and wattles made;
Nine bean-rows will I have there, and a hive for
    the honeybee,
And live alone in the bee-loud glade.

That final line, "and live alone in the bee-loud glade," may be the sweetest taste of poem-music in the English language, but why? Certainly the reverent weight of the long ooooo in "alone." But equally the "bee-loud glade," a radiant, Heavenly place for certain, as we know by the sound, the endless eeee in bee (gratitude to Indo-European ancestors for that bit of onomatopoeia, possibly rooted in *bhi,* meaning "quiver"), then the jaw dropped fully open into the rolling diphthong of "loud"—aooou—rising to the nearly endless song of the long nasal aaaaa in "glade," forcing the lips into a wide smile, sound echoing in the vibrating throat, cheeks and nasal passages at once. Yeats fought hard for this music, but the bees make it freely. Reverie of that monkish glade, his Walden Pond, his honey-coated Heaven, and its implied abundance, is where he feeds.

Today, just at the time honeybees and wild bee species are known to be dying, we have a fortunate efflorescence of poets and poetry to capture their song and plead their case.

Poet Nick Flynn, in *Blind Huber,* paints a word portrait of François Huber, the blind Swiss naturalist (1750–1831) whose fifty-year study of bees provided much of the scientific knowledge for bee behavior until the Austrian ethologist Karl von Frisch (1886–1982) published *The Dancing Bees* in 1927. Flynn the poet enters Huber's deep knowledge of bee sounds, scents, and tastes, and dares to enter the consciousness of the bees themselves—queen, worker, drone, virgin queen, robber bee—to report the joys and miseries inside the communal hive.

Two notable recent volumes of poems from the United Kingdom are expressly devoted to love of bees. Poet and beekeeper Sean Borodale's *Bee Journal* beautifully chronicles a beekeeper's year, and Poet Laureate Carol Ann Duffy's *The Bees* expresses her lyrical grief and rage at our sisters' travails. Selections from both are included here, thanks to the poets' generous permission.

Meanwhile serious observers of nature such as poet-naturalists John Caddy and Jay Salter bring us the hum of the wild bee, "some low thunder, some lingering / reverberance," as John Clare did two centuries prior in ecstatic response to the same tune.

In the end, there may be as many bee poets and poems as species of bees or bees themselves. I certainly missed many in my gathering for this hive, but I collected assiduously in the fields I could reach. Special thanks to poet-friends who took to this project like bees to nectar and collected for me many of the poems included here: Pattiann Rogers, Jim Heynen, Robert Hedin, Michael Dennis Browne, Josephine Dickinson, and Thomas R. Smith.

WHY BEES?

Ross Conrad writes in *Natural Beekeeping*: "The bee is the only creature in the animal kingdom, that I am aware of, that does not kill or injure any other being as it goes through its regular life cycle. *Apis mellifera* damages not so much as a leaf. In fact, honey bees take what they need in such a way that the world around them is improved."

During much of human history, bees and human life have been intertwined, lured by more than durable sweetness. As early as 3000 BCE, one of Pharaoh's titles was "Bee King," and beekeeping had begun at least by the seventh century BCE. Hilda Ransome notes in *The Sacred Bee in Ancient Times and Folklore* that one cathedral of the Middle Ages required thirty-four thousand beeswax candles annually for services planned during one year.

Rudolf Steiner, in a 1923 lecture on bees, goes so far as to say, "If you look at a swarm of bees, it is, to be sure, visible, but it really looks like the soul of a human being, a soul that is forced to leave its body. . . . You can really see, by looking at the escaping swarm of bees, an image of the human soul flying away from the body."

From sweet honey to practical wax to spiritual projection, the bees have been able to handle it all.

Until now. The age of synthetic fertilizers and monoculture farming creates bee food deserts, certain pesticides scramble their nervous systems, and pests such as the mite *Varroa destructor* sap their strength, all of which weaken or collapse honeybee colonies and wipe out wild bee species. That's our age. That's right now.

Poets do what we can, in our reverie, our observation, our listening, our metaphors, our occasional beekeeping, our outrage, our grief, to keep the sweetness and sting of these poetic companions alive. Scientists and citizens must do the rest.

THE BEE SCIENTISTS

This book is dedicated to entomologist Marla Spivak. Let her stand for all those scientists and beekeepers who work with the hard facts of nature, not the poets' reverie of nature. I have followed Dr. Spivak's pioneering work with bees for years, for which she has won a MacArthur "genius" grant, as she painstakingly studied the health care system of hives foundering from diseases, pesticide poisoning, and imported Asian mites. She discovered that the offspring of certain queens kept cleaner hives, therefore leaving less opportunity for mite and other infestations.

She bred a line of bees over countless generations that keep cleaner hives by removing diseased and mite-infested brood, to help revive an industry, or as she puts it, help bees "get back up on their own six feet."

Today that human industry, commercial beekeeping, reels from a complex of problems leading to "colony collapse disorder," now devastating more than 30 percent of beehives in North America and a growing number around the world. Through this anthology, I hope to call attention to Dr. Spivak and other entomologists who are the best hope to maintain populations of gentle Italian honeybees and gorgeous and productive wild bees in our lives. Emily's line, "If Bees are few," contains today a terrible poignancy.

BEE CITIZENS

The editor and poets dedicate all proceeds of this anthology, including any royalties, to the Bee Lab at the University of Minnesota, established by Dr. Spivak. If you want to know more about the condition of domestic and wild bees today, see her TED

talk, "Why Bees Are Disappearing," delivered June 12, 2013 (www
.ted.com / talks / marla_spivak_why_bees_are_disappearing
.html). At the time of this writing, it has already received more
than two million views. Then take her advice and plant bee-
friendly, pesticide-free flowering plants. Fight for sensible regu-
lation of pesticides, for the return of flowering cover crops and
lawns, for roadside flowers. And if you can, tend a hive. Tending
it, like writing a poem, takes patience and attention because the
results are always in doubt. But if you do it right, a bounty of
sweetness can endure another fifty million years.

One hundred fifty years ago Emily left behind a "simple"
lesson humanity has yet to learn:

> "Nature " is what we see—
> The Hill—the Afternoon—
> Squirrel—Eclipse—the Bumble bee— . . .
> Nature is what we know—
> Yet have no art to say—
> So impotent our Wisdom is
> To her Simplicity.

REFERENCES

Borodale, Sean. *Bee Journal*. London: Cape Poetry, 2012.
Conrad, Ross. *Natural Beekeeping: Organic Approaches to Modern
  Apiculture*. 2d ed. White River Junction, Vt.: Chelsea Green
  Publishing, 2013.
Duffy, Carol Ann. *The Bees*. London: Faber and Faber, 2013.
Flynn, Nick. *Blind Huber*. St. Paul, Minn.: Graywolf Press, 2002.
Ransome, Hilda. *The Sacred Bee in Ancient Times and Folklore*. London:
  George Allen and Unwin, 1937.
Steiner, Rudolf. *Bees*. Great Barrington, Mass.: Anthroposophic Press,
  1998.

If Bees Are Few

SHERMAN ALEXIE

In the Matter of Human v. Bee

"IF THE BEES DIE, MAN DIES WITHIN FOUR YEARS."

—*attributed to Albert Einstein, but likely stated
by an anonymous source for political reasons*

1. FOR THE PROSECUTION:

The bees are gone.
Who gives a shit?

Other insects

And animals
Can pollinate

All the flora.

We will survive
Because humans are

Adaptable.

The bees are gone.
It's a problem,

But one we'll solve
With good science
And ambition.

Certain bees

Have disappeared,
But the other

More solitary

Breeds of bee
Are still alive

And pollinating

Like porno stars.
Who needs the bees

That are too weak?

Perhaps Darwin
Should be quoted

To prove our point.

The bees are gone,
But won't stronger

Pollinators

Grow in number
And amorous

Intensity?

If you believe
In a good God,

As anyone should,

Then you must know
That God will

Create more bees

Or replace them
With something else

Equally good.

Because God is
Infallible.

2. FOR THE DEFENSE:

The bees are gone,
No one knows why.

Not even God.

Some blame cell phones.
Some blame disease.

A few blame God.

The bees are gone.
No one knows why.

If they stay gone

All flora go
Without pollen

And they perish,

Starved and godless,
Within four years.

The animals

Will soon follow
Flora to dust.

And then we die.

Nothing can stay
Because the bees

Are little gods

Who gave us grace
Bloom by bloom.

The bees are gone.

I sing this song
to bring them back,

Or say goodbye,

Or to worship
The empty sky.

3. FOR THE BEEKEEPERS:

The bees are gone.
We need new bees

Or we are fucked.

MAUREEN ASH

Swarm

I saw it in the elm above the bee yard
like a lady's softside handbag slung
from a branch, the weight of itself pulling
it into a shape as if it carried, oh, maybe
a wallet with coins for the parking meter
or some apples to eat
on the train. Ten
thousand bees of one optimistic mind, *let's
go* and they lift off, cloud, congeal
on a branch, thicken it, drip
from themselves, wait
in a satchel-shaped pulse
for the scouts to tell
them where they will go.

I studied the tree, imagined
myself climbing a ladder, saw
in hand to cut the branch, get
that swarm, re-hive it. Our longest
extension ladder, set in the bed
of the pickup truck, maybe that
might reach to where I could stretch
the saw up and at that point
I thought *let it go,* seeing myself
not as I once was, ready to climb
ladders freely, but as I am now
having heard from scouts
how far and hard
is the journey and where
it will end.

THORSTEN BACON

On Bees

Yes, we know the bee is driven to the blossom,
An arrow loosed from the bow.
Yet who taught the plum flower
That poor creature's secret name,
The hymn she is doomed to sing all day and night?

Who draws that bow with such deadly aim?
How powerless the arrow must feel!
And isn't it the target that calls the shaft to that embrace,
As the soft, warm deer's hide calls the wolf's jowls
So sweetly down?

In this same way, these words are not mine,
But yours, having only passed through this dense mass
Like moonlight through stained glass
On their way back to you.

Here they rest now, in your palms
Like an opalescent hue on worn flagstones where
Tomorrow many feet may shuffle across,
The lowered eyes passing slowly through such quailling stillness
Towards the alter with velvet, red as hibiscus,
Or an open wound,
Or my lover's lips.

ALIKI BARNSTONE

Alas

All the days since the autumn equinox
   I've been unable
      to get the word
alas
   out of my mind.
      Alas
swirled on maple leaves
   burnished by rain.
      Alas—too pretty
to be sad though it signifies sadly.
   Alas, the birds alight too briefly
      before their southern leave.
Alas, the lawn,
   monochrome emblem
      of the love of money,
a single conforming species,
   its rank's blades held aloft,
      poison-tipped,
lethal, alas, to all
   insects (except
      the few pests targeted),
lethal to little helpers
   and food progenitors.
      Alas,
too many mistake for weeds
   and eradicate our wild
      violets and clover.

I like the violet's heart-
     shaped leaves in my salad,
          shining with beads of oil.
I like to think the soil likes
     the clover to fix its nitrogen
          and the clover likes to be the grass
Walt Whitman loves, inviting us to loaf
     and hum among wildflowers
          whose names recall
daughters, home, and harvest—pincushion,
     bachelor's button, and Queen Anne's lace,
          goldenrod, cosmos, and prairie aster
sweet allysum, yarrow, and autumn joy—
     where bees intoxicated by nectar, not toxins,
          live to be our promiscuous pollinators.

WILLIS BARNSTONE

Eleven Tiny Commandments

Heaven?
Try creation

Compose
the rose

Kill?
No. Pick a daffodil

Hate?
Better climb a night cloud and lunate

Fear?
Drink a mug of cheer

Mad?
Better walk sad

Goodbye, cry
and do not die

In love?
Don't shove

Desolate?
Try chocolate

Like Emily
consult a bee

JOHN BARR

First Light

Spiders in the cold,
bees in inarticulate bunches
hang from a day's work.
Waiting for light they wait
to see what they will be.
A tree lets down
green undersides and is maple.
A window glints—
a thing of saffron
kindles with singlehood.
In the broad yard
each thing dandles
its blue, its name, its consequence.

TREE BERNSTEIN

A /B/C Scenarios

"I WOKE UP THIS MORNING IN FRENCH."

—Laure-Anne Bosselaar

A.

I dreamt of black bees swimming
in pools of nectar, seduced by fragrant yellow orchids
who held them in their bellies to fix pollen panniers—
like postage stamps to wish-you-were-here postcards

Bees as obvious as tourists in Paris sport bright orange fanny packs

B.

The long-sleeved Bee Remover posts his tired sign:
    Angry Bees Ahead!
He suits up, then busts up the bee-hive stump
as though it were just an old chifforobe

Left a mean mess
Told us he was taking them to another county
But we never saw it
Left-behind bees circle in crazy eights

C.

Between the glass and the sash a sad bumbler buzzes to be let out
The doorman ignores, then kindly summons a cab

Meanwhile, at a roof-top garden across town
a bumble bee hums into a tomato blossom's ear,
shivers her timbres & gathers her bright dust

"I woke up this morning in French."

BARRY BLUMENFELD

Boy with Honeybee Hair

Appeared walking in my
Sleep along a path through
Some woods, trailed by pilgrims;

Wonder seekers. He perched
In a crotch of a tree
And said I am a god,

A god am I. As he
Sang the honeyed verses,
His hair became a halo

Of bees, a buzzing bronze
Cloud of wingéd thoughts and
The thousand eyes they have

For their dark journeying.
Woods are dark, they need things
Like that. I am a god,

A god am I, he sang,
And the bees shimmered, and

His forehead came apart
Like a pair of wings, and
Nothing was revealed but

Air, and more bees. That's what
Death is: nothing. I came
To tell you, he buzzed. He

Was bare from his shoulders
To his waist, and below
His waist, I don't know, legs

Of an ass, or a goat,
Perhaps. I came to say,
He said, it's nothing to

Be afraid of, death. It's
A place you go to rest.

ROBERT BLY

Words Rising

—FOR RICHARD EBERHART

I open my journal, write a few
  Words with green ink, and suddenly
Fierceness enters me, stars
Begin to revolve, and pick up
Alligator dust from under the ocean.
Writing vowels, I feel the bushy
Tail of the Great Bear
Reach down and brush the seafloor.

All those deaths we lived in the sunlit
Shelves of the Dordogne, the thousand
Tunes we sang to the skeletons
Of Papua, and all those times
We died—wounded—under the cloak
Of an animal's sniffing, all these moments
Return, and the grassy nights when
We ran in the moonlight for hours.

Watery syllables come welling
Up. When a man or woman
Feeds a few words with private grief,
The shame we knew before we could
Invent the wheel, then words grow.
The old earth-fragrance remains
In the word "and." We experience
"The" in its lonely suffering.

We are bees then; our honey is language.
Now the honey lies stored in caves
Beneath us, and the sound of words
Carries what we have forgotten.
We see a million hands with dusty
Palms turned up inside each
Verb. And there are eternal vows
Held inside the word "Jericho."

Blessings then on the man who labors
In his room writing stanzas on the lamb.
And blessings on the woman who picks the brown
Seeds of solitude in afternoon light
Out of the black seeds of loneliness.
Blessings on the dictionary maker, huddled
Among his bearded words and on the setter of songs
Who sleeps at night inside his violin case.

SEAN BORODALE

24th May: Collecting the Bees

I'd say it's toiling air, high up here;
   steep with bees, and the beacon sun
burns
overlapping light, close to sundown.

Come to collect bees, our hive in parts.
Compound of fencing, stands of nucleus hives.
(Nuc,
new word.)

He just wears a veil, this farmer, no gloves
and lifts open a dribbly wax-clogged
blackwood box.
We in our whites mute with held breath.
Hello bees.
Drops four frames into our silence.

The air is like mica
ancient with thin flecks;
distance viewed through a filter of thousands.
I *am* observed.

Each box has the pulsar of its source. Porous with eyes
we wait in the spinning sun. The light is Medusa,
sugar of frayed threads; a mesh, a warp-field, all
the skin of our heads.

SEAN BORODALE

6th September: Wild Comb Notes

I have the surprise comb in September's hive:
topped between frames, great pale construction
occluded, skinned and nibbled clean
bear's-skull of paper-white wax.

I hold a knife
and cut at the block of crystalline honeyed brain.

I taste its juice; sweet gods of the evergreen
woods' taste;
crushed music, bars and epiphanies of dripping air;
aggregated cells
of each and every flower's oddness there;

this sugar-map.

My tongue swarms like a fire has been lit
clean of its obstacles.
Right on its wet hearth-slab: solar heat.

I think, each bee's six heels
may be callipers for cell's wall angles.

SEAN BORODALE

10th February: Queen

I keep the queen, she is long in my hand,
  her legs slightly pliant;
folded, dropped down, wings flat
that flew her mating flight
to the sun and back, full of spermatozoa, dronesong.
She was made mechanically ecstatic.
I magnify what she is, magnify her skews and centres.
How downy she is, fur like a fox's greyness, like a thistle's mane.
Wings perfect, abdomen subtle in shades of brittle;
her rear legs are big in the lens;
feet like hung anchors are hooks for staying on cell-rims.
Veins in her wings are a rootwork of rivers,
all echo and interlace. This is her face, compound eye.
I look at the slope of her head, the mouth's proboscis;
her thin tongue piercing is pink as cut flesh, flash glass.
Some hairs feather and split below the head.
Those eyes are like castanets, cast nets;
woman all feral and ironwork, I slip
under the framework, into the subtle.
The wing is jointed at the black leather shoulder.
I wear it, I am soft to stroke, the lower blade fans.
Third generation queen of our stock,
you fall as I turn. I hold your hunchback;
a carcase of light, no grief, part animal, part flower.

KARINA BOROWICZ

Medicine

HONEY FAIR, MOSCOW

The beekeepers have gathered at the city's edge
selling their wares from the backs of trucks
and makeshift tables
the women have wrapped flowered aprons
around their sturdy waists
with a palette knife in his brown hands
a man scoops waxy honey into jars
they are even selling bee stings
to ease arthritis or whatever else ails you
sit down with the old man who has
piercing blue wisdom in his eyes
he'll hold your bared arm gently on the upturned crate
The bees are waiting

KARINA BOROWICZ

Ruins

When they saw that the nest
of bees had been dug out of the ground
overnight by impatient claws
overnight when the bees were surely huddled
in a ball for warmth
against the hardening of October

when they saw the destruction
the amber comb strewn in pieces
on the upturned earth
the straggler bee crawling rings around
the ragged mouth of the hole
quivering feelers searching for what . . .

they didn't know why
but they were afraid

even though just the day before
they'd been gathering the last cherry tomatoes
when the bees chased them all the way
to the edge of the woods
and as they ran the ripe fruit
burst in their hands

LAURE-ANNE BOSSELAAR

Summer at the Orphanage

The bee dozes in a lily's yellow throat. July sighs
　over the convent's garth, where an old
linden blooms & bees hover
　　　　low — exhausted by the loads of pollen.

I'm only five, but exhausted too: I know longing's
　　　　weight in my lungs & legs, so I
shelter the bee there, in its buttery abundance,
　　　　my shadow a dome over the bloom.

At dusk, the chapel bells thorn the air. Swarms
　　　of uniforms flock toward that bronze authority.
I'm alone. The courtyard is empty
　　　　　　& large as absence suddenly — silent
as my mother, dark as her back & black car as she drove away,
　　　　　　flicking her ashes out the window.

Light dies. I fear the bee might get caught here —
　　　in this nunnery, like me — so I stroke its belly from
under the bloom's throat & lazy, slow, it comes out
　　　　golden as mother's jewelry.

　　　I'd like to tell you that something happened then —
that there was an epiphany, that the bee
　　　　　taught me something.
　　　　　　　But it didn't.

　　　It didn't even land in my hand or leave
its sting in me before it soared — an ashen speck —
　　　high over the walls — & was gone.

23

JILL BRECKENRIDGE

Honey

I want to say
you're as sweet as honey,

but I know that every bee
has a sting to squelch

desire, and a dense honeycomb
full of false unnerving turns

and dark dead ends, but let's
risk it, and go there anyway,

scoop up thick gold honey
with empty outstretched hands,

lift the sweetness to our mouths
and lick until we're full.

FLEDA BROWN

Bees

Here come the bees,
   the innumerable bees,
their small brains on fire
for the peanut butter and honey
of my youth, carried all morning
deep into the pathless woods
behind the cottage.
Sweat bees, dark and scant
of body—their sound *scant,*
scant. Why did I love so
to be afraid? If they sting me
now I will be glad of it,
of their sharpness, their crisp
shells, their fairy wings.

I will be glad for their partisanship,
their swarming like the waft
of a hand that knows what's best,
their conductor's grand gesture.
I will be glad even for their sticking
in thick honey, twisting
with a quiet, intimate fatality.

They have come back from
far away because I was too young
then. They move into all this
absence, into the subdivisions
named glade and hill and wood.

They are the ones who know how
to pierce the space around
my one-and-only sandwich with
their personal, pointed grief.

ROBERT BURNS

Of A' the Airts the Wind Can Blaw

Blaw, blaw ye wastin winds, blaw soft
  Among the leafy trees,
With gentle gale from hill and dale
Bring hame the laden bees.

JOHN BURNSIDE

Melissographia

I. SPRING

To make a meadow:
clover

and that kinship with the sky
we never feel until a swarm of bees

runs tidal
through a field of lavender

and perches in the spire
of witness
     not

the angels in their chill
Elysium
     and not

the curl of horseshoe crab
or spirogyra,

but hive-bees,
in their text-book instances

pure lithograph and Euclid
as they sway

through fields of happenstance
or ceaseless light

to find the echo
humming in a bone

or honeyed
in the column of a voice

so plumbline and intent,
it stands for gold

as now gives way to now,
ad infinitum.

II. SUMMER

We could have mistaken the hum
for sleep, or love,

a happiness we've never seen before,
like new rain in the grass, new light and scent

adrift among the shadows as we go
from hive to hive, in dust and goldenrod,

the blond light cutting us off
from the rest of the world

till all we can know for sure
is a cirrus of bees

and the golden aside they reserve
for the life to come.

At the edge of the woods in a 1960s
children's book from Budapest or Prague,

—the one with the wolves
and the blue house far in the meadow—

we think of ourselves again
as we might have been

had we dug our way home
through the fur of another language:

the first of the wind setting seed
in the pea-sticks and broom

and the gather of powder-blue for the only
afterlife our heaven will allow:

a waxed room, stitched
with rosemary and lime,

to set against the blet
of quince and silver.

III. AUTUMN

Someone would call it home, but there's too much
gentian at the window to be sure

and what the house is after, when it dreams
is the lemon and blur of the wind on a northern road

when evening falls and, out across the bay,
the light goes on in someone else's kitchen.

Embers of fur and spice for half a mile
of clover, they are not

the shadows of the dead, raked from the grass
and set adrift in waves of light and weather,

and nothing they can gather from the air
is theirs to keep: no breviary of rain,

no sweetened dead,
no cherish of dismay.

Their summer ends with ours,
in fog and glamour,

the light unheard-of, even as it fails:
smoke in the combs and the colourless sway of the hive

where, locked like a part of speech in the builded
city of itself,

the swarm falls silent,
stock-still in a gilt

of cornshuck and husk, a thousand-thousand-fold
its latter-day perfection, like the stars.

IV. WINTER

These are the loopholes we leave, in case
the bees return:
weeks after Halloween, the gardens white,
the windows braided with frost,
like a blueprint for purdah;

and, cold as it is, the back door stands ajar
from morning to mid-afternoon
when the children come home
with biscuits and gourds
and the hollows of Chinese lanterns.

Nothing is present, only the evening snow;
but all afternoon, we think of them drifting away,
blue in the blue of the pinewoods, white in the fog,
a final drift of perish far at sea,
Pyrrhic, indelible, frittering out like cinders.

If only we could sleep: sleep in the hive,
locked in a run of honey with our fingers
pressed to the warm, and the plummet of the mind
a shallow now: a lightness, like the dew
that settles in a mesh of columbine.

If only we could sleep, less self than vapour,
closed in a wall of citrus or alfalfa,
and listening, through salt and meadow-grass,
for those we might have answered, drifting home
to foxgloves and the memory of water.

December, now,
    and silence in the combs,
where love is something colder than we dreamed
all summer long, in rosemary and elder,
yet nothing is lost for as long as the snow blows in,
a fibre at a time, and colourless,
as bodies are, absolved of smoke and mirrors.

JOHN CADDY

Two New World Bees

Carpenter Bee

A carpenter bee mother rests on a leaf
before she takes her waxy pollen haul
to the perfectly round tunnel
she chewed into wood when she
matured and knew what she must do.
At the tunnel's deep end
she will lay an egg upon a bee bread
ball of pollen mixed with nectar,
then wall the chamber off with
a plaster of wood dust and spit.
She will end her fertile time with
a tunnel filled with cells alive
with growing daughters, safe unless
a woodpecker's spiny tongue explores.
Next spring, the youngest will be first
freed, the buzzing eldest last, so strange,
then all will know what they must do.

Leaf Cutter Bee

An oak seedling colored by autumn cold
carries leaves expertly cut by leaf cutter bees,
each cut a small moon of leaf to line or plug
a chamber of her tubular nest where she will lay
one moon-white egg and leave
bee bread enough to feed her child
through the stubborn wheel of winter.
Winged in late spring, new bees emerge.
Each summer, as trees leaf out and
Moon grows her arcs through night skies,
these little bees utter her shapes in leaves.

JARED CARTER

Landing the Bees

—FOR GEORGE P. ELLIOTT

First the bough of the apple bending; neighbors
Calling to one another in their watery voices,
None venturing close to the glittering branch.

They make way for the old bee-man, in his felt hat,
Who spreads a sheet on the grass, a white sheet
From his own bed; and with a pocket mirror

Casts the sun's image up into the swarm.
If you have walked in sleep, you know this movement
Out through air, through blossoming, down

To a new place, drawn by a brilliance in the leaves
And folded into whiteness. He takes them up
As though carrying coals. If you have wakened

Arms outstretched, you know this moment: things
Rising of their own accord are beckoning
To themselves. It is your own voice murmuring.

SHARON CHMIELARZ

Bees

those old men on motorcycles
crossing their sunlit Saharas,
the blossoms' petals, serious attachments,

buzzing

intense affairs with the biggest and boldest,
the pale, northern hibiscus called hollyhock,
the red threads in a peony's mound,
the yucca's white bells, hanging silent,

buzzing

what a whisper
could never be—ponderous,
voluminous bulge and pulse,
Russian fragility,

buzzing

in summer,
eponymous natter
between fuse and hummer.

LUCILLE CLIFTON

earth

here is where it was dry
when it rained
and also
here
under the same
what was called tree
it bore varicolored
leaves children bees
all this used to be a
place once all this
was a nice place
once

SAMUEL TAYLOR COLERIDGE

Inscription for a Fountain on a Heath

This Sycamore, oft musical with bees,—
Such tents the Patriarchs loved! O long unharmed
May all its aged boughs o'er-canopy
The small round basin, which this jutting stone
Keeps pure from falling leaves! Long may the Spring,
Quietly as a sleeping infant's breath,
Send up cold waters to the traveller
With soft and even pulse! Nor ever cease
Yon tiny cone of sand its soundless dance,
Which at the bottom like a Fairy's Page,
As merry and no taller, dances still,
Nor wrinkles the smooth surface of the Fount.
Here twilight is and coolness: here is moss,
A soft seat, and a deep and ample shade.
Thou may'st toil far and find no second tree.
Drink, Pilgrim, here; here rest! And if thy heart
Be innocent, here too shalt thou refresh
Thy spirit, listening to some gentle sound,
Or passing gale or hum of murmuring bees!

LORNA CROZIER

Angel of Bees

The honeycomb
that is the mind
storing things

crammed with sweetness,
eggs about to hatch—
the slow thoughts

growing wings and legs,
humming memory's
five seasons, dancing

in the brain's blue light,
each turn and tumble
full of consequence,

distance and desire.
Dangerous to disturb
this hive, inventing clover.

How the mind wants
to be free of you,
move with the swarm,

ascend in the shape
of a blossoming tree—
your head on the pillow

emptied of scent and colour,
winter's cold indifference
moving in.

The Sacrament of the Bees

After my father died, no, I mean *later,*
after my mother died, there was the problem
of family treasure no one wanted.

What does it mean that we tossed out
a whole wall of boxes—a lifetime's work—
of his eloquent handwritten sermons?

Brothers, sister, we all divided things up,
chose which inheritances
we would carry forth. The thing is

somewhere in the midst of all that judgment
those penned words
may have held the sweetest and best

of that complex man. Still, it seems
none of us wanted to shoulder
the weight of all those lessons.

One morning in August I watched
from the chicken coop roof, tar
softening beneath my knees,

as my father opened the battered beehive
behind the apple tree in the garden:
an act I only got to witness once.

My brother was with his chickens
while my mother moved slowly
through morning chores, so only

an idle six-year-old was there to watch
as Father emerged from the barn,
white sleeves rolled down, bleached

trousers tucked, and his veiled helmet
like something my mother
would wear to church. August,

and even so early in the morning
the heat made my father appear
to shimmer in shades of white

against the corn as he squeezed a cloud
from the tip of the tin bee-smoker
then pried loose the hive's great lid.

Did amber flow that day
or was the colony already lost?
Whether he spoke then to the living

or the dead, he was murmuring something
to that hive, something that is lost now,
something we are poorer without, and freer.

With Flowers

South winds jostle them,
Bumblebees come,
Hover, hesitate,
Drink, and are gone.

Butterflies pause
On their passage Cashmere;
I, softly plucking,
Present them here!

The bee is not afraid of me

The bee is not afraid of me,
I know the butterfly;
The pretty people in the woods
Receive me cordially.

The brooks laugh louder when I come,
The breezes madder play.
Wherefore, mine eyes, thy silver mists?
Wherefore, O summer's Day?

Possession

Did the harebell loose her girdle
   To the lover bee,
Would the bee the harebell hallow
Much as formerly?

Did the paradise, persuaded,
Yield her moat of pearl,
Would the Eden be an Eden,
Or the earl an earl?

Two Worlds

It makes no difference abroad,
  The seasons fit the same,
The mornings blossom into noons,
And split their pods of flame.

Wild-flowers kindle in the woods,
The brooks brag all the day;
No blackbird bates his jargoning
For passing Calvary.

Auto-da-fe and judgment
Are nothing to the bee;
His separation from his rose
To him seems misery.

The Bee

Like trains of cars on tracks of plush
I hear the level bee:
A jar across the flowers goes,
Their velvet masonry

Withstands until the sweet assault
Their chivalry consumes,
While he, victorious, tilts away
To vanquish other blooms.

His feet are shod with gauze,
His helmet is of gold;
His breast, a single onyx
With chrysoprase, inlaid.

His labor is a chant,
His idleness a tune;
Oh, for a bee's experience
Of clovers and of noon!

EMILY DICKINSON

Could I but ride indefinite

Could I but ride indefinite,
As doth the meadow-bee,
And visit only where I liked,
And no man visit me,

And flirt all day with buttercups,
And marry whom I may,
And dwell a little everywhere,
Or better, run away

With no police to follow,
Or chase me if I do,
Till I should jump peninsulas
To get away from you,

I said, but just to be a bee
Upon a raft of air,
And row in nowhere all day long,
And anchor off the bar,
What liberty! So captives deem
Who tight in dungeons are.

EMILY DICKINSON

The pedigree of honey

The pedigree of honey
Does not concern the bee;
A clover, any time, to him
Is aristocracy.

EMILY DICKINSON

To make a prairie it takes a clover and one bee

To make a prairie it takes a clover and one bee,
One clover, and a bee.
And revery.
The revery alone will do
If bees are few.

B

When I finally donned the long black and yellow striped dress
and jumped on the bus for a flight with my first lover
you had recently rejoined the beekeepers' association
you first hived with fifty years before.

Then a year or two later you gave up—beaten
by mum's reaction. She nearly died
from a few bee stings. Was it any surprise
when one sibling stabbed your bee books with a knife,
the other, scalded and scabbed, was left with a waxen abdominal
      scar?

In the thirties when you started at the Old Mill bee club
you surely knew my lover's bee-mad father.
You, in your twenties, living close, were devastatingly handsome
and single. Did you meet his father's wife?

My lover was born soon after.
Was that your secret?
Was that why you kept your head down?
Why you married so late?

When you put on your white coat and veil
you seemed quite different. You made me a nice-girl
dress before I swarmed.
It billows green on the line behind you in the flower-drunk
      garden.

When did you eat honey from the carcass of a lion?
She gave you away. She had the bairn. And she died.
These are just the facts. You knew how to keep a queen satisfied.
You knew how to see the eggs she was laying.

Which one am I? I have been fertilized
by human seed. I saw you. What was wrong
with the black honey of the year I was born?
Unctuous and rich could you have allowed me a taste.

Since my maiden flight I have toiled in darkness.
You are always worrying the bees are about to swarm.
Daddy thinks the bees are going to swarm Mummy says.

The hot wax pours from my ears,
the silencer of the drum.
And yet the structure and the membranes
are formed to perfection in every comb.

I remain in the hive.
I shuffle from cell to cell.
I plant my eggs in the triune base—
bee, bea, beata, bu, bit, bite, bitte, bijou, beautiful . . .

CAROL ANN DUFFY

Bees

Here are my bees,
 brazen, blurs on paper,
besotted: buzzwords, dancing
their flawless, airy maps.

Been deep, my poet bees,
in the parts of flowers,
in daffodil, thistle, rose, even
the golden lotus; so glide,
gilded, glad, golden, thus—

wise—and know of us:
how your scent pervades
my shadowed, busy heart,
and honey is art.

CAROL ANN DUFFY

Ariel

Where the bee sucks,
 neonicotinoid insecticides
in a cowslip's bell lie,
in fields purple with lavender,
yellow with rape,
and on the sunflower's upturned face;
on land monotonous with cereals and grain,
merrily,
merrily;
sour in the soil,
sheathing the seed, systemic
in the plant and crops,
the million acres to be ploughed,
seething in the orchards now,
under the blossom
that hangs
on the bough.

CAROL ANN DUFFY

Virgil's Bees

Bless air's gift of sweetness, honey
from the bees, inspired by clover,
marigold, eucalyptus, thyme,
the hundred perfumes of the wind.
Bless the beekeeper

who chooses for her hives
a site near water, violet beds, no yew,
no echo. Let the light lilt, leak, green
or gold, pigment for queens,
and joy be inexplicable but there
in harmony of willowherb and stream,
of summer heat and breeze,

each bee's body
at its brilliant flower, lover-stunned,
strumming on fragrance, smitten.

For this,
let gardens grow, where beelines end,
sighing in roses, saffron blooms, buddleia;
where bees pray on their knees, sing, praise
in pear trees, plum trees; bees
are the batteries of orchards, gardens, guard them.

54

RALPH WALDO EMERSON

The Humble-Bee ·

Burly, dozing humble-bee,
  Where thou art is clime for me.
Let them sail for Porto Rique,
Far-off heats through seas to seek;
I will follow thee alone,
Thou animated torrid-zone!
Zigzag steerer, desert cheerer,
Let me chase thy waving lines;
Keep me nearer, me thy hearer,
Singing over shrubs and vines.

Insect lover of the sun,
Joy of thy dominion!
Sailor of the atmosphere;
Swimmer through the waves of air;
Voyager of light and noon;
Epicurean of June;
Wait, I prithee, till I come
Within earshot of thy hum,—
All without is martyrdom.

When the south wind, in May days,
With a net of shining haze
Silvers the horizon wall,
And, with softness touching all,
Tints the human countenance
With a color of romance,
And, infusing subtle heats,

Turns the sod to violets,
Thou, in sunny solitudes,
Rover of the underwoods,
The green silence dost displace
With thy mellow, breezy bass.

Hot midsummer's petted crone,
Sweet to me thy drowsy tone
Tells of countless sunny hours,
Long days, and solid banks of flowers;
Of gulfs of sweetness without bound
In Indian wildernesses found;
Of Syrian peace, immortal leisure,
Firmest cheer, and bird-like pleasure.
Aught unsavory or unclean
Hath my insect never seen;
But violets and bilberry bells,
Maple-sap, and daffodels,
Grass with green flag half-mast high,
Succory to match the sky,
Columbine with horn of honey,
Scented fern, and agrimony,
Clover, catchfly, adder's-tongue
And brier-roses, dwelt among;
All beside was unknown waste,
All was picture as he passed.

Wiser far than human seer,
Yellow-breeched philosopher!
Seeing only what is fair,
Sipping only what is sweet,
Thou dost mock at fate and care,
Leave the chaff, and take the wheat.
When the fierce northwestern blast

Cools sea and land so far and fast,
Thou already slumberest deep;
Woe and want thou canst outsleep;
Want and woe, which torture us,
Thy sleep makes ridiculous.

HEID E. ERDRICH

Intimate Detail

Late summer, late afternoon, my work
interrupted by bees who claim my tea,
even my pen looks flower-good to them.
I warn a delivery man that my bees,
who all summer have been tame as cows,
now grow frantic, aggressive, difficult to shoo
from the house. I blame the second blooms
come out in hot colors, defiant vibrancy—
unexpected from cottage cosmos, nicotianna,
and bean vine. But those bees know, I'm told
by the interested delivery man, they have only
so many days to go. He sighs at sweetness untasted.

Still warm in the day, we inspect the bees.
This kind stranger knows them in intimate detail.
He can name the ones I think of as *shopping ladies*.
Their fur coats ruffed up, yellow packages tucked
beneath their wings, so weighted with their finds
they ascend in slow circles, sometimes drop, while
other bees whirl madly, dance the blossoms, ravish
broadly so the whole bed bends and bounces alive.

He asks if I have kids, I say not yet. He has five,
all boys. He calls the honeybees his girls although
he tells me they're *ungendered workers*
who never produce offspring. Some hour drops,
the bees shut off. In the long, cool slant of sun,
spent flowers fold into cups. He asks me if I've ever
seen a *Solitary Bee* where it sleeps. I say I've not.

The nearest bud's a long-throated peach hollyhock.
He cradles it in his palm, holds it up so I spy
the intimacy of the sleeping bee. Little life safe in a petal,
little girl, your few furious buzzings as you stir
stay with me all winter, remind me of my work undone.

HEID E. ERDRICH

Stung

She couldn't help but sting my finger,
clinging a moment before I flung her
to the ground. Her gold is true, not the trick
evening light plays on my roses.
She curls into herself, stinger twitching,
gilt wings folded. Her whole life just a few weeks,
and my pain subsided in a moment.
In the cold, she hardly had her wits to buzz.
No warning from either of us:
she sleeping in the richness of those petals,
then the hand, my hand, cupping the bloom
in devastating force, crushing the petals for the scent.
And she mortally threatened, wholly unaware
that I do this daily, alone with the gold last light,
in what seems to me an act of love.

EARL OF ESSEX (ROBERT DEVEREUX)

The Buzzeinge Bee's Complaynt

1

It was a time when sely bees coulde speake,
And in that time, I was a sely bee,
Who suckt on time, vntill my hart did breake,
Yet neuer found the time would fauoure me:
Of all the swarme I only could not thriue,
Yett brought I wax and honye to the hyue.

2

Then thus I buzzd when time no sapp would giue:
Why is this blessed tyme to me so drye?
Sith in this time the busy drone doth liue,
The waspe, the worme, the gnatt, the butter-flye:
Mated with Greife I kneelèd on my knees
And thus complaynèd to the kinge of bees.

3

God graunt my Leige Thye time maye neuer ende,
And yet vouchsafe to heare my playnte of Time,
W^{ch} euery fruyctlesse fly hath found a frende,
And I caste downe, when Attomyes doe clyme:
The kinge replyed but this, 'peace peevyshe bee,
Borne thou art to serue the time, the tyme not thee.

4

'The tyme not thee': the worde clipt short my winge
And made me worme-like stoope that once did flye:
Awefull regard disputeth not with kinges,
Receues repulse, and neuer asketh whye:
Then from the tyme, a tyme I me with drewe,
To sucke on hen bane, hemlocke, netteles, rewe.

5

Whilst all the swarme in sunshine taste the rose;
On blacke fearnse roote I seeke and sucke my bayne;
Whilst on the eglantayn the reste repose
To light on wormewoode leaues they me constrayne;
Hauinge to much they still repyne for more
And cloyed with swetnesse surfeyte on their store.

6

Swolne fatt wth feasts full merryly they passe
In sweetenod clusters fallinge on a tree,
Where findinge me to nybble on the grasse
Some scorned, some mused, and some did pyty me.
And some me enuied, and whispered to the kinge
Some must be still, and some must haue no sting.

7

Ar bees waxt waspes, and spyders, to afflycte? *are*
Doe hony bowells make the spiritts galle?
Is this the iuce of flowers to flie suspecte?
Is't not enough to treade on them that fall?
What stinge hath Patience but a single greife
That stings nought but it self wth out releefe.

8

Sad Patience, that attendeth at the dore,
And teacheth wise-men thus conclude in schooles:
Patience I am, and therfore must be poore:
Fortune bestowes her riches not on fooles.
Great kinge of bees that righteth euery wronge
Listen to Patience in her dyinge songe.

9

I cannot feede on fenell like some flyes
Nor flye to euery flower to gather gayne:
My appetyte wayts on my Prince's eyes
Contented with contempt, and pleasèd with all payne:
And yet expectinge for a happye hower
When shee may say the bee may sucke a flower.

10

Of all my greefes that most my patience grate
Ther's one that fretteth in the hyest degree;
To see some catterpillers brede of late
Croppinge the flowers that should sustayne the bee.
Yet smilèd I, for that the wisest knowes
Moaths eate the cloth, cankers consume ye rose.

11

Once did I see by flyinge in the feilde
Foule beasts to browse upon the lyllys fayer;
Vertue nor Beautye could no succoure yelde.
All's prouender to the asse but the ayere:
The partyall worlde takes very carelesse heede
To giue them flowers that would on thistles feede.

12

Thus only I must drayne Egiption flowers,
Findinge no sauore; bitter sapp they haue.
And seeke out rotten tombes, the dead mens bowers
And byte on Lotus growinge by the graue.
If this I cannot haue, as heppelesse Bee
Wishèd, Tabacco I will flee to thee!

13

What thoughe thou dye my loungs in deepest blacke?
A morninge habite sutes a sable harte:
What thoughe thy fumes, sound memorys dos cracke?
Forgetfulnes is fittest for my smarte.
O vertuous fume, let it be graued on oke
That words, hope, witts, and all the world, is smoke.

14

Ffiue years twice tould, wth promases perfum'd,
My hope-stuffte heede was caste into a slumber;
Sweete dreams of golde; on dreames I then presum'd
And 'mongst the bees thought I was in the number.
Late wakinge, hyues, hopes, had made me vayne,
Was but Tabacco stupyfied my brayne.

JOHN EVANS

The Bees

With merry hum the Willow'd copse they scale,
The Fir's dark pyramid, or Poplar pale;
They waft their nut-brown loads exulting home,
That form a fret-work for the future comb,
Caulk every chink where rushing winds may roar,
And seal their circling ramparts to the floor.

DIANE FAHEY

Bees

Bees then.
  I haven't thought of you

for months, except when
pegging out the clothes,

feet shifting
in clover where you work.

Pollen bearers
who serve fertility,

you are the ones
I've most wished to celebrate:

guardians of this hive—
building and humming,

storing and culling—
the shapers who know

the ways of the queen-muse
with her gorgeous abundance,

the sterility she inflicts
as she lies being nurtured.

Do you remember
the golden honeycomb

of Daedalus,
the twinned bee brooch

from Knossos,
Mycenae's beehive tombs?

You dance through these images
of opulence, ceremonious

balance, death; you are there
at the birth of poets,

buzzing and swarming
near the mouth

to instil
the gift of eloquence.

Your own voice declares
a pitch of knowledge,

expresses
your life's music,

provides the ground bass
for other voices.

In close-up,
daemonically hairy,

you are a transformer,
part of the bedrock of things.

LAWRENCE FERLINGHETTI

Alienation: Two Bees

I came upon them in the cabin—
  the angry one at the window
    and the old bent one on the bed
  the one at the window buzzing & buzzing
        beating its wings on the window
           beating the pane
  the one on the bed
    the silent one with the bent frame
        alone on the counterpane
I didn't mean to kill them
  but the one in the window
      wouldn't be waved
        back to his hive
  The door was open and he knew it
    and flew in for a moment
    and then flew back
      away from his community
Something had alienated him
    and he would not go back
  or was it perhaps
      the wounded one on the bed
      who kept him
I tried to get him to fasten onto
      a crumpled page
       of the local news
    but he would not
And I must have hurt him doing that
      for he fell on the bed

and died in an instant
stretching out his legs
or arms
as if to his comrade or lover
who crawled a quarter-inch toward him
and then hunched up
into a very small furry ball
and was still
and would not move again
As all at once outside
the hive hummed louder
with a million mild conformists
with wild antennas bent

Not one flew out to wake the dead

No messenger was sent

NICK FLYNN

Workers (Attendants)

Nights we lie beside her, our mouths
at her belly, counting

her breaths, the buzz, the gathering, long
done. We all began
inside her, like those lined up

inside her now, mere
idea of ourselves
unborn. We wash her body

ceaselessly, move our tongues
until all her hairs loosen. She

roams the brood, finds
another empty cell

& fills it. Morning comes &
she calms us, keeps us inside
until the dew burns off. This sodden

world. All winter
we huddled around her, kept her
warm. Those on the outside, those
farthest from her, died

first, their legs
gripped the others like a shawl.

NICK FLYNN

Hive

What would you do inside me?
you would be utterly

lost, labyrinthine

comb, each corridor identical, a
funhouse, *there*, a bridge, worker

knit to worker, a span
you can't cross. On the other side

the queen, a fortune of honey.

Once we filled an entire house with it,
built the comb between floorboard

& joist, slowly at first, the constant

buzz kept the owners awake, then
louder until honey began to seep

from the walls, swell
the doorframes. Our gift.

They had to burn the house down
to rid us.

NICK FLYNN

Blind Huber (iii)

Sometimes bees, the glittering

curtain they form, cling to my face,

& the moment before knowing

I can imagine them a leaf, able to be

brushed away, but they

hold on, their tongues

seek each pore,

as if my cheek offered nectar, they move

delicately, caress &

shade, as if not threatening

to flood my eyes.

NICK FLYNN

Queen

Net suit &
smoking cup, you reek fear.
If we fight back, or if there isn't

enough, you seek me out with gloved fingers
to crush my head. When we sting

you scream. We know why

you carry our white boxes
to the edge of the alfalfa, to the figs

& raspberries. You take our honey
because we let you. We pollinate the fields

because we are the fields.

STUART FRIEBERT

Supersedure

1

Under the notch in the old willow, home
of many a hive, I read workers kill the old

queen when a new queen emerges to mate,
one of only two ways the colony "requeens."

Swarming's the other m.o.: numbers of queens
are bred by being fed royal jelly, a protein-laden

glob the hypopharygeal gland in mature workers
exudes. I look up to clear my eyes, the meadow's

suddenly alive with a hovering swarm, so I put
my book down, quickly net my head, start running.

2

There's dead silence now; night's curtain's fallen.
I'd be lying if I said I caught up with the swarm to

return to for any honey the bees might share without
retribution. I'd just wanted to be somewhere else, no

more craving for conflict, knowledge of the efficient
world. My heart's softened. Now when I cut off a twig

I don't cut the air with a swish, begin to break into words.
Really, I'd do anything you told me to if it didn't cause

trouble, begin chores hoping not to finish them; what would
spread out over less than a page. "Breathing's my hobby, man,"

an old friend on Death Row writes. No one's jokes are as rich.
I just hope I'll be the first to arrive out of air at the last hive.

ROSS GAY

Ode to the Beekeeper

—FOR STEPHANIE SMITH

who has taken off her veil
and gloves and whispers to the bees
in their own language, inspecting the comb-thick
frames, blowing just so when one or the other alights
on her, if she doesn't study it first—the veins
feeding the wings, the deep ochre
shimmy, the singing—just like in the dreams
that brought her here in the first place: dream
of the queen, dream of the brood chamber,
dream of the desiccated world and sifting
with her hands the ash and her hands
ashen when she awoke, dream of honey
in her child's wound, dream of bees
hived in the heart and each wet chamber
gone gold. Which is why, first,
she put on the veil. And which is why,
too, she took it off.

EAMON GRENNAN

Up Against It

It's the way they cannot understand the window
they buzz and buzz against, the bees that take
a wrong turn at my door and end up thus
in a drift at first of almost idle curiosity,
cruising the room until they find themselves
smack up against it and they cannot fathom how
the air has hardened and the world they know
with their eyes keeps out of reach as, stuck there
with all they want just in front of them, they must
fling their bodies against the one unalterable law
of things—this fact of glass—and can only go on
making the sound that tethers their electric
fury to what's impossible, feeling the sting in it.

BARBARA HAMBY

The Language of Bees

The language of bees contains 76 distinct words for stinging,
distinguishes between a prick, puncture, and mortal wound,
elaborates on cause and effect as in a sting made to retaliate,
    irritate, insinuate, infuriate, incite, rebuke, annoy,
    nudge, anger, poison, harangue.
The language of bees has 39 words for queen—regina apiana,
    empress of the hive, czarina of nectar, maharani of the ovum,
    sultana of stupor, principessa of dark desire.

The language of bees includes 22 words for sunshine,
Two for rain—big water and small water, so that a man urinating
    on an azalea bush in the full fuchsia of April
    has the linguistic effect of a light shower in September.
For man, two words—roughly translated—"hands" and "feet,"
    the first with the imperialistic connotation of beekeeper,
    the second with the delicious resonance of bareness.
All colors are variations on yellow, from the exquisite
    sixteen-syllable word meaning "diaphanous golden fall,"
    to the dirty ochre of the bitter pollen
    stored in the honeycomb and used by bees for food.

The language of bees is a language of war. For what is peace
    without strife but the boredom of enervating day-after-day,
    obese with sweetness, truculent with ennui?
Attack is delightful to bees, who have hundreds of verbs
    embracing strategy, aim, location, velocity:
    swift, downward swoop to stun an antagonist,
    brazen, kamikaze strike for no gain but momentum.

Yet stealth is essential to bees, for they live to consternate
    their enemies, flying up pant legs, hovering in grass.
No insect is more secretive than the bee, for they have two
    thousand words describing the penetralia of the hive:
    octagonal golden chamber of unbearable moistness,
    opaque tabernacle of nectar,
    sugarplum of polygonal waxy walls.

The language of bees is a language of aeronautics,
    for they have wings—transparent, insubstantial,
    black-veined like the fall of an exotic iris.
For they are tiny dirigibles, aviators of orchard and field.
For they have ambition, cunning, and are able to take direct aim.
For they know how to leave the ground, to drift, hover, swarm,
    sail over the tops of trees.

The language of bees is a musical dialect, a full, humming
    congregation of hallelujahs and amens,
    at night blue and disconsolate,
    in the morning bright and bedewed.
The language of bees contains lavish adjectives
    praising the lilting fertility of their queen:
    fat, red-bottomed progenitor of millions,
    luscious organizer of coitus,
    gelatinous distributor of love.
The language of bees is in the jumble of leaves before rain,
    in the quiet night rustle of small animals,
    for it is eloquent and vulgar in the same mouth,
    and though its wound is sweet it can be distressing,
    as if words could not hurt or be meant to sting.

TOM HENNEN

Outside Work

On these autumn days when even the sunshine is cold,
I feel happily lonesome as the wild bee that comes looking
for one last flower before the snow. I move drowsily through the
warm spots in the day. My muscles, too, are stiff if I drift into the
shadows. The sudden chill makes me shudder. I move through
the floating spider webs and reach a clearing in the sunlight
where the earth itself is about to fall asleep in its own daydream.
In the dream the bee and I are both children in the same family.
We have never left home. Everything tastes like honey.

JIM HEYNEN

The Man Who Talked to His Bees

The beekeeper was always talking. He sounded as if he had as
much to say as his bees in apple blossom season. But all he
talked about was what he was doing.

Now I'm moving this hive over just a bit. Now I'm checking
the angle toward the sun. There. Now I'm walking to the clover
field to see what we have this year.

He went on like this all day long, day after day, while the bees
went on buzzing about their business as if he didn't exist.

One day a blind pastor was walking through the country
hoping to hear a voice from heaven. When he walked past the
beekeeper's place, he heard a strange voice over the buzzing of
the bees.

The blind pastor stopped and listened more carefully. The
sound of the bees was like the golden pillars of heaven in his
mind, and the voice of the beekeeper was like the Lord Himself
descending from heaven.

I am listening, said the blind pastor. Now he heard the voice
of the beekeeper again, saying, I am going to wipe the sweat from
my forehead. There.

The blind pastor trembled, fearing that he was a cause for the
Lord's perspiring. Falling to his knees, he said, Have I been such a
labor to Thee, Lord?

My nose itches, said the beekeeper. I'm going to move my
wrist slowly up to it and rub it a bit. There.

Now the blind pastor feared he was an offensive odor to the
sensitive nostrils of the Lord.

Does my earthly body offend Thee, Lord?

Just then the beekeeper heard the blind pastor and turned to
see who it was. The sight of the blind pastor kneeling along the

road with his hands stretched toward the sky was so strange that the beekeeper stopped talking for the first time in many days.

With that, several bees came down on him and stung him, since the beekeeper never wore any netting to protect himself. The beekeeper screamed and swore in pain, then ran as fast as he could to find some mud before the swelling began.

The blind pastor, hearing the ungodly commotion, sprang to his feet, vowing never to wander through the country again. He started walking slowly back toward town where every Sunday he preached two sermons.

The beekeeper resolved to mend his ways also and never to stop talking in the presence of his bees again, no matter how great the distraction.

The bees went on buzzing in their usual way, since, for them, this was a very busy time of the year.

SELIMA HILL

Elegy for the Bee-God

Stingless bees
were bred in tree hollows
for beeswax and honey.
Every year, in the month
called Tzec, the bee-keepers
played their raspadores
and danced across the fields
with bells and ribbons
round their feet, to honor
the fat bee-god, who buzzed
in the heated air
to their music.
He lived in a gold house
in the hotlands, and drank
cocoa sweetened with honey.

All's quiet now, it's June,
and he's not here, the late,
the long-forgotten bee-god,
who sped on zigzag wings
across the sky to the faithful.

Cross-eyed, bejeweled
and tattooed, drumming
his fluffy yellow feet
on the tree hollows,
he gave the bees new hope,
and cocoa sweetened with honey.

If ever I find him—thin,
justly offended, dead
in the dry chaparral—
I will put jade beads
and honey on his tongue,
and wrap him in a shroud
of wings, and loop his neck
with pearls from Guatemala;
I will light him candles
of beeswax, bringing sleep,

and he will rest in the shade
of the First Tree,
and wait for me there—
humming a tune, and drinking
cocoa sweetened with honey.

BRENDA HILLMAN

In Summer,
Everything Is Something's Twin

—FOR CH

Tell your mother's first syllable the moth
to bring its trigon to the doorframe . . .
the universe is speeding up,
electrons swallowed by the rose—
you work so hard, too-hard-too-hard.
Humans have made a disaster but
—but what, sister?
—but nothing, pencil. tttap-tap.
Such a short season between dogwood
& tiger-lily. Sunscreen sinks
between hairs on your arm. Western yew
[*Taxus brevifolia*] requests a canopy . . .

People come here for their bit of joy,
they gather in western towns,
radicals growing weed in the woods, makers
of quilts & clouds, loggers, keepers
of the sick with their hounds; they
rest on weekends, in bars,
for love without reason or ledger;
Castor & Pollux sink in the cougar's cry . . .
in a month or so, the sky will swallow Gemini—

Hurry now, for the hive is ill,
the cedar branch bows low as the wagon passes

& earth lies in the long earth bed . . .
Plenty of accidents come your way
but today you are otherwise,
today you train yourself to be safe, to work
as Billy has trained the little horse—

JANE HIRSHFIELD

Bees

In every instant, two gates.
One opens to fragrant paradise, one to hell.
Mostly we go through neither.

Mostly we nod to our neighbor,
lean down to pick up the paper,
go back into the house.

But the faint cries—ecstasy, horror?
Or did you think it the sound
of distant bees,
making only the thick honey of this good life?

KEVIN HOLDEN

Bees

Bees in Virgil—something silver and secret,
  Like lightning over the land
Or striking a plum tree on some dried hill.

Bees in Frost: light jumping off the back of a flower—yellow jackets
And a grasshopper too—always wet and alive since it's spring—
White faces peeking over stacks of new hay.

Bees also
In Crane,
Strange and mechanical, mud wasps,
A corset of wires,
The buzz
Of a tiny iron machine,
Thunderstorm coming
On a dark afternoon.

Dickinson knew the smallest bees,
Tiptoeing along the edge of her desk,
Until she got an idea and suddenly stood,
Knocking the table, the bee taking off
Into the night she was rapidly opening,
Catching a glimpse at the end of the world
Of a white rocking chair
And, behind it, circumference,
An enormous black pine, blue sky,
The little bee obliterated by white-yellow light.

O'Hara saw a bee,
Following a long line of salt through the air,
Buzzing new purple gold, a little blurry,
Wavering, like a doubloon in the azure, under the water.

And Mandelstam's bees
Wore the thin wings of time,
Every one silent and enormously still,
Staring at him from the stone of the page.

KOBAYASHI ISSA

Haiku

secluded house—
the bees also memorize
the way back

(translated by David G. Lanoue)

My Bees: An Allegory

O bees, sweet bees!" I said, "that nearest field
Is shining white with fragrant immortelles.
Fly swiftly there and drain those honey wells."
Then, spicy pines the sunny hive to shield,
I set, and patient for the autumn's yield
Of sweet I waited.
When the village bells
Rang frosty clear, and from their satin cells
The chestnuts leaped, rejoicing, I unsealed
My hive.
Alas! no snowy honey there
Was stored. My wicked bees had borne away
Their queen and left no trace.
That very day,
An idle drone who sauntered through the air
I tracked and followed, and he led me where
My truant bees and stolen honey lay.
Twice faithless bees! They had sought out to eat
Rank, bitter herbs. The honey was not sweet.

NAOMI JACKSON

Prairie Bees

It's cold on the prairie in winter.

Damn cold.

Come summer we covet
the bounty of the garden,
squash and apples and berries,
cabbages for kraut,

and a little extra sweetness
to hold us through the winter.
So we got some bees

and they hummed in the orchard and berry patch,
and wandered the flowering vines.
They sang to us of summer heat,
of melons fat in the sun and honey to sweeten December nights.

It's cold on the prairie in winter.
Can a hive hold on through dark nights
and sun dog days?

Can a hive stay warm when knife-edged winds
sling drifts against its walls?

We didn't know,
so we put the hive in the cellar,
in the corner behind the apple barrel
and the crocks of kraut.

Next day, there's a bee
helping itself to the jam pot,
then two, then a dozen,
loving strawberries in December.

One lights on Ma's African violet,
and then there's a whole parade
buzzing up the cellar stairs.

The young kids find fly swatters
and apply them to the jam pot
while the older ones help wrestle the hive
up and out behind the barn.

We cover the whole darn thing with hay bales
while the wind whistles our hats off.

Back in the kitchen we warm up
with jam on toast and tea
sweetened with honey.

GEORGE JOHNSTON

Ecstatic

When basswood blows   bees make in it,
mill in midsummer   myriad pillage;
probing to pull out   pollen and sweetness
they swing sure-foot   searching of mouth.
A massive murmur   moves through the basswood
and breathes blissful   her bosom kiss.
Caressed queen   she crowns the season,
her senses swarming   in shared ferment.

SUSAN DEBORAH KING

Prayer

You fill with an anguish.
It swells you. It strains
like a bud against its sepals.
you fear its power,
the explosion of its color.
You want to purse yourself,
repel its surge
and drive this dreadful sap
back into the ground,
but you let it burst,
allow the petals of your pain to fan out,
layer and array themselves
around your tender center.
The air is charged
with ultraviolet, and this
is what draws the Bee:
that all out opening up,
the quick of you disclosed.
She works you for all you're worth,
bagging your dust, drinking your blood,
until, drunk,
She rubs some of your male into your female,
doing the sex that brings a seed out of this death.
The rest she converts to viscid gold.

RUDYARD KIPLING

The Bee-Boy's Song

Bees! Bees! Hark to your bees!
'Hide from your neighbours as much as you please,
But all that has happened, to us you must tell.
Or else we will give you no honey to sell!'

A maiden in her glory,
Upon her wedding-day,
Must tell her Bees the story,
Or else they'll fly away.
Fly away—die away—
Dwindle down and leave you!
But if you don't deceive your Bees,
Your Bees will not deceive you.

Marriage, birth or buryin',
News across the seas,
All you're sad or merry in,
You must tell the Bees.
Tell 'em coming in an' out,
Where the Fanners fan,
'Cause the Bees are justabout
As curious as a man.

Don't you wait where trees are,
When the lightnings play;
Nor don't you hate where Bees are,
Or else they'll pine away.
Pine away—dwine away—
Anything to leave you!
But if you never grieve your Bees,
Your Bees'll never grieve you.

D. H. LAWRENCE

Flapper

Love has crept out of her sealed heart
As a field-bee, black and amber,
Breaks from the winter-cell, to clamber
Up the warm grass where the sunbeams start.

Mischief has come in her dawning eyes,
And a glint of coloured iris brings
Such as lies along the folded wings
Of the bee before he flies.

Who, with a ruffling, careful breath,
Has opened the wings of the wild young sprite?
Has fluttered her spirit to stumbling flight
In her eyes, as a young bee stumbleth?

Love makes the burden of her voice.
The hum of his heavy, staggering wings
Sets quivering with wisdom the common things
That she says, and her words rejoice.

DAVID LEE

On Finding a Drone Bee and a Painted Lady Butterfly in the Same Claret Cup of Cactus Blossom

"HOW RELUCTANTLY
THE BEE EMERGES FROM DEEP
WITHIN THE PEONY."

—*Basho*

The red light's on,
lady's on the table

and the first john
is the Apostle Paul, confused celibate,
lost drone, missionary

from the Queen of Heaven
who thinks he's found
the Holy Grail, the flying nun

on the brink of damnation,
a fallen angel in the honky-tonk

primed for an afternoon wallow,
blown off course
and dumped in the bordello

knee deep in agua miel,
his personal challenge from God.

JAMES P. LENFESTEY

Honey

In Pharaoh's tomb, honey,
thick and sweet,
to journey with him to the Afterworld
which is, for me and you
the Here and Now, wandering
with our tongues this viscous gold
distilled from furtive visits
to a million random flowers
five thousand years ago
that deserves today a hundred
Nobel prizes.

Honey is food the way poetry
is food, sweet as a child's wounded smile
is sweet, complex the way fine wine's
complex, enrapturing the entire mouth,
with a sticky, lasting finish.

Sometimes honeyed words in ancient tongues
crystallize inside old stone books
'til translators heat them to their fluid state
and we sit down, you and I, to talk
and dine with sweet young Pharaoh.

JAMES P. LENFESTEY

Blaming the Bee

A small boy, popular enough on the playground
   at his first school, beginning to sense
the new life there, running the bases at recess,
scoring a run.

Why then did the yellowjacket single him out?
Harass him and his sandwich?
Resist his waving hand, then flailing arms,
advance with a stinger sword?

And why did he cry in front of the entire school,
then run, one block and then another,
until home appeared twenty blocks later,
and run up the stairs and hide under the bureau?

Where his mother found him and sweetly asked
and he said he was stung by a bee
but he knew he wasn't stung by a bee
but by his tears, and it was shameful to blame the bee

and shameful to cry at all
and shameful to cry in front of all the others
and shameful to run all the way home
and shameful to hide under the bureau
and shameful that his mother was so kind
and shameful that his sister teased him
and shameful that his dad at dinner said nothing
and shameful to this day that he blamed the bee.

NATHANIEL "MAX" LENFESTEY

Beard of Bees

I'm walking down the street
and the bushes are so sweet-
smelling that I'm practically
wearing a beard of bees.
The buzz is quite intense,
but they have no interest
in me.

My father used to dream
of keeping bees
though he kept them mostly
chasing honey
trapped in his beard.

Funny how a walk
can write a poem.
How a poem can take you
from a beard of bees
to your father's beard
sticky with honey.

NATHANIEL "MAX" LENFESTEY

Her Sting

As a tender stalk of nine,
I watch the fuzzy
bumbling of bees wearing

Black and yellow war paint
buzzing through the garden,
pollen-dusted workers
mining flowers.

Mom is in the kitchen
gazing at unfinished chores,
wondered where her worker bee
could be?

Her sting is gentler
than a drop of honey.

DIANE LOCKWARD

Invective against the Bumblebee

Escapee from a tight cell, yellow-streaked,
sex-deprived sycophant to a queen,
you have dug divots in my yard
and like a squatter trespassed in my garage.

I despise you for you have swooped down
on my baby boy, harmless on a blanket of lawn,
his belly plumping through his orange stretch suit,
yellow hat over the fuzz of his head.
Though you mistook him for a sunflower,
I do not exonerate you,
for he weeps in my arms, trembles, and drools,
finger swollen like a breakfast sausage.
Now my son knows pain.
Now he fears the grass.

Fat-assed insect! Perverse pedagogue!
Henceforth, may flowers refuse to open for you.
May cats chase you in the garden.
I want you shellacked by rain, pecked by shrikes,
mauled by skunks, paralyzed by early frost.
May farmers douse your wings with pesticide.
May you never again taste the nectar
of purple clover or honeysuckle.
May you pass by an oak tree just in time
to be pissed on by a dog.

And tomorrow may you rest on my table
as I peruse the paper. May you shake
beneath the scarred face of a serial killer.
May you be crushed by the morning news.

ANTONIO MACHADO

Song

By the flowering sierra
the broad sea bubbles.
In my honeycomb of bees
are tiny grains of salt.

(translated by Willis Barnstone)

ANTONIO MACHADO

Proverbs and Songs

Bees, singers
not for the honey but for the flowers.

(translated by Willis Barnstone)

ANTONIO MACHADO

Last Night, As I Lay Sleeping

Last night, as I was sleeping,
  I dreamt—marvelous error!—
that a spring was breaking
out in my heart.
I said: Along which secret aqueduct,
Oh water, are you coming to me,
water of a new life
that I have never drunk?

Last night, as I was sleeping,
I dreamt—marvelous error!—
that I had a beehive
here inside my heart.
And the golden bees
were making white combs
and sweet honey
from my old failures.

Last night, as I was sleeping,
I dreamt—marvelous error!—
that a fiery sun was giving
light inside my heart.
It was fiery because I felt
warmth as from a hearth,
and sun because it gave light
and brought tears to my eyes.

Last night, as I was sleeping,
I dreamt—marvelous error!—
that it was God I had
here inside my heart.

(translated by Robert Bly)

BRUCE MacKINNON

The Bees

One day the bees start wandering off, no one knows why.
First one doesn't come back, and then another and another,
until those who are supposed to stay and guard the hive, those
who are making the royal jelly and feeding it to the queen,
those who form different parts of the great brain, must
put down what it is they are doing and go off in search—
having no choice, not if the hive is going to survive,
and where do they go, each one vanishing, never to be seen
again, off wandering in the wilderness, having forgotten
how, forgotten what it was they were after, what it was
that gave meaning, having known it at one time, now
a veil drawn. Is it that each one is a cell, a brain cell,
and now they're failing one by one, plaque to Alzheimer's,
or the way the cells in the esophagus will begin to mimic
the stomach if the acid is too intense, if you're sleeping
and the valve won't close, a lifetime of eating and drinking
the wrong things, those cells compensating, trying
their best, but opening the door to those other cells,
the wild ones, the ones that call those bees, out there,
somewhere, lost, having nowhere to return at night,
their search for nectar fruitful, their small saddlebags full,
but no one to go home to, no home, no memory of home,
it's as if they'd stumbled into some alternate world,
one looking like ours but just a glass width different,
just a fraction of sunlight different, the patient waking up,
finding herself wandering, someone leading her back
to bed, but there is no bed. Confusion of the hive,
they call it, and the hive dies, each bee goes down,

each light goes out, one by one, blinking out all over town,
seen from a great height as the night ages, darkens,
as you're parked in your car with your own true love,
until it's just you two and the stars, until it's just you.

The Necklace

Take, from my palms, for joy, for ease,
A little honey, a little sun,
That we may obey Persephone's bees.

You can't untie a boat unmoored.
Fur-shod shadows can't be heard,
Nor terror, in this life, mastered.

Love, what's left for us, and of us, is this
Living remnant, loving revenant, brief kiss
Like a bee flying completed dying hiveless

To find in the forest's heart a home,
Night's never-ending hum,
Thriving on meadowsweet, mint, and time.

Take, for all that is good, for all that is gone,
That it may lie rough and real against your collarbone,
This string of bees, that once turned honey into sun.

(translated by Christian Wiman)

THOMAS McCARTHY

Foraging Honey-Bees

Such stories brought home by the foraging honey-bee: the world
Is too corporate now, the nitrogen-rich call-centre has grown
Fatigue, greenish scum covers the breath in hayfield and stream.
Listen now, the stars are beginning to tell us their stories too;
The very-far stars, that is, signals picked up, no doubt,
By the faltering bee-hives in Ned Lonergan's farm. Only this
Very morning we were astonished to hear of the vacant hive,
The second one, where the bees had left without giving notice;

The hive, now, becomes a little apartment block of cells for rent.
I thought of the clever ones in the European Space Centre
And how they've just picked up a new celestial music,
A signal with a watery cadence from a distant sister Earth.
Twenty light years from Lonergan, Cappoquin, a bee-hive
In a planet that is dedicated to peace has just received
Its exhausted colonists: bees that heard, long before astro-physics,
Of fields far away, of dandelions, clean rivers, white Dutch clover.

PAULA MEEHAN

The January Bee

who comes to the winter flowering shrub,
grief in his empty pouches, who sups
alone in the stilled garden this dusk:

I would have missed him only I stopped
mid-argument to catch the moonrise
over the wet roofs of the suburb

and caught him at work deep in the musk,
shaking the bells of the scarce blossoms,
tolling our angers, ringing in peace.

ROBERT MORGAN

Bees Awater

You find one drinking at the creek,
scratching and drinking
before takeoff.
He lifts back
and takes aim, firing homeward.
That's the moment to get your sighting,
get the direction and slant of climb
and you'll be looking right at the tree
on the ridge above
where the honey hangs inside
like cells of a battery
charged with sweetness.
The whole tree has the hum of a transformer.
Bees bubble, circling
 like electrons.

Though excited as before a holdup
and hot from the long climb,
you drop the ax
and wait for dark.

ROBERT MORGAN

Honey

Only calmness will reassure
the bees to let you rob their hoard.
Any sweat of fear provokes them.
Approach with confidence, and from
the side, not shading their entrance.
And hush smoke gently from the spout
of the pot of rags, for sparks will
anger them. If you go near bees
every day they will know you.
And never jerk or turn so quick
you excite them. If weeds are trimmed
around the hives they have access
and feel free. When they taste your smoke
they fill themselves with honey and
are laden and lazy as you
lift the lid to let in daylight.
No bee full of sweetness wants to
sting. Resist greed. With the top off
you touch the fat gold frames, each cell
a hex perfect as a snowflake,
a sealed relic of sun and time
and roots of many acres fixed
in crystal-tight arrays, in rows
and lattices of sweeter latin
from scattered prose of meadows, woods.

ROBERT MORGAN

Moving the Bees

When the owner of the place died,
the keeper of a row of hives
on hillside or orchard middle,
before the body was carried
out, before even a wreath hung
on the door or any other
sign of mourning, the bees had to
be moved. In January cold
or March wind or summer dark the gums
must be shifted an inch, a finger
width, from the place the keeper left
them, or the colonies would die
or swam and leave, as though all ten
thousand humming workers in combs
and crystal lattices, compacting
honey from the trees and fields in
morning music, must register
the fine displacement of a death,
shift in sensitive alignment
with the sun and seasons, down to
the least egg and cell and sparkling
atom of sweetness, to start
the new dispensation in an
altered relationship to house
and woods and prevailing air,
and show the changing order now
the old one had passed away—
and the universe was moved.

LISEL MUELLER

Life of a Queen

1. CHILDHOOD

For two days her lineage is in doubt,
then someone deciphers the secret message.
They build a pendulous chamber
for her, and stuff her with sweets.

Workers keep bringing her royal jelly.
She knows nothing of other lives,
about digging in purple crocus
and round dances in the sun.

Poor and frail little rich girl,
she grows immense in her hothouse.
Whenever she tries to stop eating,
they open her mouth and force it down.

2. THE FLIGHT

She marries him in midair;
for a moment
he is ennobled, a prince.

She gives the signal
for their embrace;
over too soon. O, nevermore.

Bruised, she drags herself from
his dead body,
finds her way back exhausted.

She is bathed, curtains are drawn.
Ten thousand lives
settle inside her belly.

Now to the only labor she knows.
She remembers
nothing of him, or their fall.

3. THE RECLUSE

They make it plain
her term is over.
No one comes;
they let her starve.

The masses, her children,
whip up sweets
for a young beauty
who is getting fat.

Nothing to do.
Her ovaries paper,
her sperm sac dust,
she shrivels away.

A crew disassembles
her royal cell.
Outside, a nation
Crowns its queen.

AMY NASH

Not Just a Question of Fertility

First, having read the book
of myths, I prepare my own
concoction for uncovering the pattern
in the silver serving dish
of deadly love. Four pomegranate seeds,
several spoonfuls of honey

from the few colonies remaining
on this side of the mud-laden river.
Is it mites, disease, fumes
from SUV's burdening old steel
bridges on the south side? Your absence
has gone through me the way

no drink
could. Once
there was a beekeeper.

Everyone assumed he was mute. He kept his mouth
closed, kept to his bees, ten stings
a day was acceptable, twenty,
too much. Maybe he should have spoken
up. He could talk
when he wanted to—he had a mouth. When his bees died,

he crossed the river in a silver varnished skiff. When it rained,
the boat sang a pounding rhyme. There's no escape,
the land's been raped, we're all going down,
we're all going to drown. The beekeeper rowed on—

town overlapping town, winding down river
to the banks of mine. When I first saw him, he me, when
     I coaxed him

to dry land, spoke to him
with the motion of my limbs, quiet lips,
I did not know
he would become you. I did not know you
would only stay long enough for the clouds to drain.
I did not know this would be your last—this honey
to be eaten.

PABLO NERUDA

Ode to the Bee

Multitude of the bee!
It enters and exits from
the crimson, the blue,
the yellow,
from the softest
softnesses on earth:
it enters
a corolla
in a hurry,
on business,
leaves
with a gold suit
and a number of
yellow boots.

Perfect
from its waist,
its abdomen striped
with dark bands,
its little head
always
worried
and its
wings
new-made from water:
it enters
through every fragrant window,
it opens
doors of silk,
it pierces the bridal chambers

of the most fragrant love,
it bumps
into
a
drop
of dew
as if into a diamond,
and from every
house it visits,
it takes
mysterious
honey,
rich and heavy
honey, thick scent,
liquid light that falls in big drops,
until to its
collective
palace
it returns,
and in the gothic parapets
it deposits
the product
of flower and flight,
seraphic, secret, nuptial sun!

Multitude of the bee!
Sacred
elevation
of unity,
throbbing
academy!

Sonorous
numbers
buzz
as they work
the nectar
and swiftly

transfer
drops
of ambrosia:
it's the siesta
of summer in the green
solitudes
of Osorno. Above,
the sun drives its spears
into the snow,
volcanoes sparkle,
the land is
wide
as the seas,
space is blue,
but
there is something
that trembles, it's
the burning
heart of summer,
the heart of
multiplied honey,
the murmuring
bee,
the crackling
honeycomb
of flight and gold!

Bees,
pure laborers,
workers of
the gothic arch,
refined, flashing
proletarians,
perfect,
reckless militias
that in combat attack
with suicidal stingers,

buzz,
buzz over
the gifts of the earth,
family of gold,
multitude of the wind,
shake fire
from the flowers,
thirst from the stamens,
sharp
thread of smell
that unites the days,
and propagate
honey
passing over
the humid continents,
the most distant islands
of the western sky.

Yes:
let the wax raise
green statues,
let the honey
spill over
infinite
tongues,
and let the ocean be
a hive,
the earth
a tower and robe
of flowers,
and the world
a waterfall,
a comet's tail,
an unending
coming forth
of honeycombs!

(translated by Dan Bohnhorst)

AIMEE NEZHUKUMATATHIL

Bee Wolf

Not a bee. Not a wolf. A *wasp*.
Once I saw one try to lift a lizard
off a wall. The lizard did nothing, only
held its pink suction toes a bit tighter.
But after a few stings, the lizard's

tongue flicked furious, and it fell.
I've felt it too. When a man you love
won't love you back, almost nothing
can pry your sticky fingers from a phone,
even if you just want to hear the pause

in his voice you know so well—so well
you could pick out his exact breath
in a darkened room full of men. A mother
bee wolf teaches its babies well. To dig
an underground cell of soil almost

a yard deep, she carries a pebble at a time
back to the surface in her shiny mandibles.
She paints a white spot with her furry legs
on the place where her baby should start
digging once it's ready to try the lavender air.

That baby will soon find a lizard of her very own.
At least she has a direction—I am sick
with the lack. I need a mark, a tattoo
etched on the arch of my foot, telling me
what to hold, clutch only what is mine.

JOAN NICHOLSON

Antics of Bees

astonishing the asters
    buzzing bougainvillea
        cavorting with coreopsis

day dreaming among dahlias
    enlightening elderberries
        fraternizing with freesia

gamboling in the gladioli
    hovering over honeysuckle
        indulging Indian paint brush

jumping into jonquils
    kissing Kaffir lilies
        lolling among lobelia

mesmerizing magnolias
    nuzzling nasturtiums
        ogling olallieberries

pirouetting with peonies
    quickening hearts of quince
        ruminating over roses

swarming around snapdragons
    trifling with tulips
        undulating the undergrowth

visiting violets
    wandering around water lilies
        exciting the xylia

yearning for yarrow
    zealously
        pursuing zinnias

NAOMI SHIHAB NYE

Honeybee

Dipping into the flower zone
Honey stomach plump with nectar

Soaking up directions
Finding our ways in the dark

Fat little pollen baskets
Plumping our legs

You had no idea, did you?
You kept talking about

That wheelbarrow
And chicken

Round dance
Waggle dance

Only 5 species of honeybee
Among 20,000 different bee species

Out there in the far field
Something has changed but

You don't know what it is yet
And everything depends

On us

NAOMI SHIHAB NYE

Bees Were Better

In college people were always breaking up.
We broke up in parking lots,
beside fountains.
Two people broke up
across a table from me
at the library.
I could not sit at that table again
though I did not know them.
I studied bees, who were able
to convey messages through dancing
and could find their ways
home to their hives
even if someone put up a blockade of sheets
and boards and wire.
Bees had radar in their wings and brains
that humans could barely understand.
I wrote a paper proclaiming
their brilliance and superiority
and revised it at a small café
featuring wooden hive-shaped honey-dippers
in silver honeypots
at every table.

NAOMI SHIHAB NYE

Pollen

Sometimes in the mornings
a sense of knowing tickles my windows,

mechanical thud outside,
gears shifting, engine waking up

like a bee doing its waggle dance
in front of the hive.

Even if I don't know what the yellow machine
means, exactly, it companions me.

Man in a bucket, examining high light,
repairing lines nibbled by a squirrel.

The world's at work in the hopeful hour,
things put together

won't be blown apart,
dissolve or disappear.

Did you know bees ventilate their homes
by hovering outside and fanning their wings?

Light passes through thinking.
Helps us find the field again.

Happiness

In the afternoon I watched
the she-bear; she was looking
for the secret bin of sweetness—
honey, that the bees store
in the trees' soft caves.
Black block of gloom, she climbed down
tree after tree and shuffled on
through the woods. And then
she found it! The honey-house deep
as heartwood, and dipped into it
among the swarming bees—honey and comb
she lipped and tongued and scooped out
in her black nails, until

maybe she grew full, or sleepy, or maybe
a little drunk, and sticky
down the rugs of her arms,
and begun to hum and sway.
I saw her let go of the branches,
I saw her lift her honeyed muzzle
into the leaves, and her thick arms,
as though she would fly—
an enormous bee
all sweetness and wings—
down into the meadows, the perfection
of honeysuckle and roses and clover—
to float and sleep in the sheer nets
swaying from flower to flower
day after shining day.

Honey at the Table

I t fills you with the soft
essence of vanished flowers. It becomes
a trickle sharp as a hair that you follow
from the honey pot over the table

and out the door and over the ground,
and all the while it thickens,

grows deeper and wilder, edged
with pine boughs and wet boulders,
pawprint of bobcat and bear, until

deep in the forest you
shuffle up some tree, you rip the bark,
you float into and swallow the dripping combs,
bits of the tree, crushed bees—a taste
composed of everything lost, in which everything
lost is found.

JOE PADDOCK

A Sort of Honey

Soft golden bees, filled with fire,
storm round the hive, and helpless
in our dream of the sweet,
we are stung again and again.

The world *will* take
our measure. If our days
are not hard enough
on their own, our desire
will rise to sting us.

Yes, we suffer here
and purify and ripen,
and a sort of honey grows
in the wax of our dying cells.

LINDA PASTAN

The Death of the Bee

"THE DEATH OF WILD BEE POPULATIONS
HAS BECOME WIDESPREAD . . ."

—news report

The biography of the bee
is written in honey
and is drawing
to a close.

Soon the buzzing
plainchant of summer
will be silenced
for good;

the flowers, unkindled
will blaze
one last time
and go out.

And the boy nursing
his stung ankle this morning
will look back
at his brief tears

with something
like regret,
remembering the amber
taste of honey.

The Bee Meeting

Who are these people at the bridge to meet me? They are
the villagers—
The rector, the midwife, the sexton, the agent for bees.
In my sleeveless summery dress I have no protection,
And they are all gloved and covered, why did nobody tell me?
They are smiling and taking out veils tacked to ancient hats.

I am nude as a chicken neck, does nobody love me?
Yes, here is the secretary of bees with her white shop smock,
Buttoning the cuffs at my wrists and the slit from my neck to my
knees.
Now I am milkweed silk, the bees will not notice.
They will not smell my fear, my fear, my fear.

Which is the rector now, is it that man in black?
Which is the midwife, is that her blue coat?
Everybody is nodding a square black head, they are knights in
visors,
Breastplates of cheesecloth knotted under the armpits.
Their smiles and their voices are changing. I am led through a
beanfield.

Strips of tinfoil winking like people,
Feather dusters fanning their hands in a sea of bean flowers,
Creamy bean flowers with black eyes and leaves like bored hearts.
Is it blood clots the tendrils are dragging up that string?
No, no, it is scarlet flowers that will one day be edible.

Now they are giving me a fashionable white straw Italian hat
And a black veil that molds to my face, they are making me one
of them.
They are leading me to the shorn grove, the circle of hives.

Is it the hawthorn that smells so sick?
The barren body of hawthorn, etherizing its children.

Is it some operation that is taking place?
It is the surgeon my neighbors are waiting for,
This apparition in a green helmet,
Shining gloves and white suit.
Is it the butcher, the grocer, the postman, someone I know?

I cannot run, I am rooted, and the gorse hurts me
With its yellow purses, its spiky armory.
I could not run without having to run forever.
The white hive is snug as a virgin,
Sealing off her brood cells, her honey, and quietly humming.

Smoke rolls and scarves in the grove.
The mind of the hive thinks this is the end of everything.
Here they come, the outriders, on their hysterical elastics.
If I stand very still, they will think I am cow-parsley,
A gullible head untouched by their animosity,

Not even nodding, a personage in a hedgerow.
The villagers open the chambers, they are hunting the queen.
Is she hiding, is she eating honey? She is very clever.
She is old, old, old, she must live another year, and she knows it.
While in their fingerjoint cells the new virgins

Dream of a duel they will win inevitably,
A curtain of wax dividing them from the bride flight,
The upflight of the murderess into a heaven that loves her.
The villagers are moving the virgins, there will be no killing.
The old queen does not show herself, is she so ungrateful?

I am exhausted, I am exhausted—
Pillar of white in a blackout of knives.
I am the magician's girl who does not flinch.
The villagers are untying their disguises, they are shaking hands.
Whose is that long white box in the grove, what have they
        accomplished, why am I cold.

SYLVIA PLATH

Stings

Bare-handed, I hand the combs.

The man in white smiles, bare-handed,
Our cheesecloth gauntlets neat and sweet,
The throats of our wrists brave lilies.
He and I

Have a thousand clean cells between us,
Eight combs of yellow cups,
And the hive itself a teacup,
White with pink flowers on it,
With excessive love I enameled it

Thinking "Sweetness, sweetness."
Brood cells gray as the fossils of shells
Terrify me, they seem so old.
What am I buying, wormy mahogany?
Is there any queen at all in it?

If there is, she is old,
Her wings torn shawls, her long body
Rubbed of its plush—
Poor and bare and unqueenly and even shameful.
I stand in a column

Of winged, unmiraculous women,
Honey-drudgers.
I am no drudge
Though for years I have eaten dust
And dried plates with my dense hair.

And seen my strangeness evaporate,
Blue dew from dangerous skin.

Will they hate me,
These women who only scurry,
Whose news is the open cherry, the open clover?

It is almost over.
I am in control.
Here is my honey-machine,
It will work without thinking,
Opening, in spring, like an industrious virgin

To scour the creaming crests
As the moon, for its ivory powders, scours the sea.
A third person is watching.
He has nothing to do with the bee-seller or with me.
Now he is gone

In eight great bounds, a great scapegoat.
Here is his slipper, here is another,
And here the square of white linen
He wore instead of a hat.
He was sweet,

The sweat of his efforts a rain
Tugging the world to fruit.
The bees found him out,
Molding onto his lips like lies,
Complicating his features.

They thought death was worth it, but I
Have a self to recover, a queen.
Is she dead, is she sleeping?
Where has she been,
With her lion-red body, her wings of glass?

Now she is flying
More terrible than she ever was, red
Scar in the sky, red comet
Over the engine that killed her—
The mausoleum, the wax house.

LIA PURPURA

Bee

For once I was not bent
on denying the worst scenario
but listened to the bee
get louder as it came closer.
I was still as the rumble moved
into my chest and the machinery
of its wings passed over.

*

The bee kept changing direction, midair,
and the sound diminished or grew close randomly.
I've seen the brightest yellow flicker
do the same in a wet, green field
—take one sip, reverse itself,
and look for some fresh thing because
it so loved the idea of abundance.

*

But I was only part of the abundance.
And who else would I be
so adorned, but clearly
an attractive thing to it,
a singular sweetness
willing to think
like an adornment.

*

Then I saw myself as I was—
not nearly what it wanted.
I did not grow, like the rose,

dangerous and inviting
steps to my heart, and my heart
was not perfect—hidden,
dusty, and small.

★

In place of what it wanted,
I would do. And I saw
my two wild arms
in the air, waving,
not knowing how to say
I was more than that,
in its language.

JERI REILLY

Honey

September air is headier
than June, and I am drunk as Emily—
in the backyard, even this patch of city
is pungent with the history
of begotten fruit and flower,
the garden besotted
at the end of the love-making months.

Survey this exuberance of dying flowers—
the bee balm stems stand blackened,
they are in their cycle still
next to these old flames,
powdery yarrow falls for sun,
but the yellow cone flowers, fresh blown,
are dizzying summer's last bees.

Label on the honey jar to come:
Last flowers, sweet bite.

JAMES SILAS ROGERS

Bumblebee in the Basement

They come in through limestone
cracks in the foundations
of old homes like this,
to nest in musty basements.
I went to find a crowbar downstairs
and found a bee, big as a wine cork,
doggedly batting
the floorboards and joists.

I emptied a jar of nails,
cupped it over her buzzing form.
The jar became a snow-globe
whirring with frustration.
I've heard it said that, on paper,
a bee can't really fly. No one
told this one: she was adamant in her
will to ascend.

Outside, I turned the jar over.
Like a spark flying upward,
she rose, her recent captivity
cast off as if it never happened.
      She lifted toward the sky
like a balloon released
from a child's grasp, then halted,
suddenly, on an apple blossom.

And I had forgotten
why I needed that crowbar.

PATTIANN ROGERS

Service with Benediction

Chunk honey, creamed honey, buckwheat
honey on buckwheat bread—like glass lanterns,
there's enough concentrated summer sun caught
in these jars of comb honey to give us
ample light to travel by on a winter night.

Sesame breads, sausage breads, almond
breads, sweet panettones, cassava cakes
and millet cakes, all are laid out
on the table before me beside these bowls
of molasses honey and heather honey, wild
wood honey gathered by wild bees, hallows
of honey, orisons of bulging loaves.

So I eat sun and earth by the slice
and spoonful, suck yeast breads soaked
in alfalfa honey, dip crusts dripping
from the dish to my mouth, lick gold
sugar from my fingers. I swallow
pure flower syrup brought from the sky,
chew the kneaded spike and germ of fields
and gardens. Surely I become then
all the arabesques of bee dances,
and the cultures of beebread balls rolled
from nectar pollen. I comply easily
with the lean of heady buds and grasses
waxing and waning at their cores
sunk in the earth.

Two gifts, I heard the temple bakers say,
when, for immortality, the priests immersed
his dead body naked before burial
in a cistern of amber honey.

Allow me now in the fullness of this morning
to consume enough clover honey and white
wheat fire to see my way clearly
through the cold night coming.

PAUL B. ROTH

Illusory

Existing
  as though
a honeybee's
buzz

was some
flexible
neon string
threading
its systematic
flight along

there
still remains
a blood
swollen sun
ahead

squinting
and blurring
the unending

sting
of its vision
in our watery
eyes

When Grapes Turn to Wine

When grapes turn
to wine, they long for our ability to change.

When stars wheel
around the North Pole,
they are longing for our growing consciousness.

Wine got drunk with us,
not the other way.
The body developed out of us, not we from it.

We are bees,
and our body is a honeycomb.
We made
the body, cell by cell we made it.

(version by Robert Bly)

JAY SALTER

Bee Hum

Each spring there's a faint roar near the porch as the bees
   visit diligently all day the canyon gooseberry bush.
The tiny fuchsia-like flowers, thorn-guarded and ivory-
      white hang from their red-lipped base. They must harbor
a sweet nectar indeed. All day the dreamy sound pervades,
      low thunder whorls in the gooseberry shade. And yet, eyes
         closed,
lounging under its green cloud, listening, you can distinguish
      several different species of bees, their tones, the different
wing vibrations, as they hum and drone, hover and bumble
      by all day. Even when one bee is leaving, always
another is winging in, thundering in from some distance,
      stitching its life for some moments in the gooseberry's shade.
Listening within that green dusk one might wonder if
      sound more than scent or sight draws each wanderer in.

JAY SALTER

Night Hum

The bees emerge in the morning from their hives just
    underground.
    A few at first, humming out busily, or buzzing at the lip,
orienting themselves to the sun. And then, one by one,
    they leave their neat nests, their slumber and their troves
      of honey,
and set briskly about their daylong domesticities,
    traveling, gathering a dark wild honey for their hives.
They arrive at our garden just at our departure for work,
    while we linger on the steps or by the car with a kiss,
or hmm and buss in passing, quickening our good-byes.
    We spend long hours gathering apart, not home till the bees
are gone. Not home even later. But homing. As later, one hears
    around the house, outside the porch, over the roses,
under the uncertain stars, some low thunder, some lingering
    reverberance, some dark wild humming under the eaves.

JAY SALTER

Non-Colonizing Native Bees

Small wild bees hovering in situ inhabit the meadow:
   nodes, tiny coals, hardly a third of an inch
in length with brownish-golden fur or down—conjuring
     the faintest halo of sun—hum. Burning motes
floating over enumerable blue elfin flowers
     stay placed, spaciously constellate galaxies of grass.
They tuck their legs up as they ride, bodies thrust forward,
     blurred wings in their unwavering attention describe
parabolas. They seem to select their airy perches not
     necessarily for the nectar which their long needle-like
       proboscises
enchantingly serve. But as vantage for mates or their solitary
     nests.
     They're extremely fierce toward their fellows, as if one
     and only
one placement were fitting, with any intrusion jealously
     challenged, a jotting or quick scribble finally deciding it.

ROBERT SAMAROTTO

Happy Hour at the Prickly Pear Saloon

You can always find them there
buzzing away the hours
—the regulars
the plumed hair of their odd legs
powdered with pollen
—noses deep in the nectar.

For these workers
it is the best of times
no clocks
no assembly lines
no unions
only drinking and pollinating
—dances in the arms of golden stamens

All day they toil until the wee hours
when they begin droning
songs of honey gathering
risqué ballads of cross pollination
sad bee music for those lost to the desert sea

They harmonize
until the last flower has collapsed
then punch out
rev-up their small engines and at a luff
float out wing to wing
through the fiery spines of the prickly pear
past the daggers of the Spanish bayonets
navigating over ways grown dark
home to their amber world
home to the grave housekeeper
who lives within.

FIONA SAMPSON

Winter Bees

Every year
the weak January sun
brings bumblebees
nudging and thudding against the wood
of my work shed—
which must smell good, some old pine sweetness
soft in the grain
under the blue cracked paint, a blue
miracle sky.
Still, this banality moves us—
a small spring
resurrection, in the time
just before spring.

What tender precision
directs each bee
to our recurring conversation,
its compass set
by the sun's enormous arc?
The bee Christ
wears his crown of gilt and mourning,
mnemonic
of the winter swarm. *Out
of strength came forth
sweetness.* Our dark
hearts are hives.

WILLIAM SHAKESPEARE

Ariel's Song

Where the bee sucks, there suck I:
In a cowslip's bell I lie;
There I couch when owls do cry.
On the bat's back I do fly
After summer merrily.
Merrily, merrily shall I live now
Under the blossom that hangs on the bough.

—*from* The Tempest, *act V, scene 1*

JO SHAPCOTT

I Tell the Bees

He left for good in the early hours with just
one book, held tight in his left hand:
The Cyclopedia of Everything Pertaining
to the Care of the Honey-Bee; Bees, Hives,
Honey, Implements, Honey-Plants, Etc.
And I begrudged him every single et cetera,
every honey-strainer and cucumber blossom,
every bee-wing and flown year and dead eye.
I went outside when the sun rose, whistling
to call out them as I walked towards the hive.
I pressed my cheek against the wood, opened
my synapses to bee hum, I could smell bee hum.
"It's over, honies," I whispered, "and now you're mine."

JO SHAPCOTT

The Threshold

I waited all day for tears and wanted them, but
there weren't tears. I touched my lashes and
the eyewater was not water but wing and fur
and I was weeping bees. Bees on my face,
in my hair. Bees walking in and out of my
ears. Workers landed on my tongue
and danced their bee dance as their sisters
crowded round for the knowledge. I learned
the language too, those zig-zags, runs and circles,
the whole damned waggle dance catalogue.
So nuanced it is, the geography of nectar,
the astronomy of pollen. Believe me,
through my mouth dusted yellow
with their pollen, I spoke bees, I breathed bees.

JO SHAPCOTT

The Hive

The colony grew in my body all that summer.
The gaps between my bones filled
with honeycomb and my chest
vibrated and hummed. I knew
the brood was healthy, because
the pheromones sang through the hive
and the queen laid a good
two thousand eggs a day.
I smelled of bee bread and royal jelly,
my nails shone with propolis.
I spent my days freeing bees from my hair,
and planting clover and bee sage and
woundwort and teasel and borage.
I was a queendom unto myself.

JO SHAPCOTT

Going About with the Bees

I walked to the city carrying the hive inside me.
The bees resonated my ribs: by now
my mouth was wax, my mouth was honey.
Passers-by with briefcases and laptops
stared as bees flew out of my eyes and ears.
As I stepped into the bank the hum
increased in my chest and I could tell the bees
meant business. The workers flew out
into the cool hall, rested on marble counters,
waved their antennae over paper and leather.
"Lord direct us." I murmured, then felt
the queen turn somewhere near my heart,
and we all watched, two eyes and five eyes,
we all watched the money dissolve like wax.

CCD

My body broke when the bees left,
became a thing of bones
and spaces and stretched skin.
I'd barely noticed
the time of wing twitch
and pheromone mismatch
and brood sealed in with wax.
The honeycomb they
left behind dissolved
into blood and water.
Now I smell of sweat and breath
and I think my body cells
may have turned hexagonal,
though the bees are long gone.

JO SHAPCOTT

The Sting

When the wild queen leads the swarm
into the room, don't shut the door on them,
don't leave them crawling the walls, furniture
and books, a décor of moving fuzz. Don't go off
to the city, alone, to work, to travel underground.
The sting is no more *apis mellifera,* is a life
without honey bees, without an earful of buzz
an eyeful of yellow. The sting is no twin
waving antennae breaking through
the cap of a hatching bee's cell. The sting
is no more feral hive humming in the stone
wall of the house, no smell of honey
as you brush by. No bees will follow, not one,
and there lies the sting. The sting is no sting.

SU SMALLEN

Buddha, Lily

Buddha, bathing, contemplates the island his tummy makes
   on the island is a lake his belly button makes
in the lake is Buddha, bathing, contemplating the island his
      tummy makes
on the island is a lake his belly button makes and so Buddha
      moves

into the center that is not-center, and because it is not-center,
      we call it center.
In the center around the lake grow cattails, at the foot of the
      cattails lay pollen
at the foot of the pollen are the feet of sticky staircases
climbing up the pleated petals that form the freckled lily.

Opening like a twelvefold plate of petal, not-petal,
the lily-plate is the biography of Buddha in 12 chapters
the 12th chapter, being, of course, Complete Openness.

The lily is to feed the bee.
When the lily becomes transparent
chapters fall, not-lily remains;

another bud reaches, fattens, mindfully
explodes one silken cell at a time
to feed the bee, happiness.

THOMAS R. SMITH

The Queen in Winter

"UNLIKE HONEYBEES, WHICH SURVIVE BY HUDDLING
TOGETHER IN THE WINTER, BUMBLEBEES ONLY
LIVE FROM SPRING TO FALL, LEAVING ONLY
THE QUEEN TO LIVE THROUGH THE WINTER."

—*Chris Hardman's Ecological Calendar*

She nods in her empty banquet hall,
crown heavy on her sleep-heavy head.
They are all gone, the soldiers and midwives,
the blond-bearded boys and fleet, golden girls,
floating tapers that animated summer,
snuffed not by darkness but by cold.

The flowers were sweet, but only a little
less lasting than the burly pollen-
wranglers that hummed and sailed the hot breezes.
Now earth hardens, streams flow to a standstill,
without and within, the castle door stiffens
against white winds that bend the stems low.

In her brain the year dwindles to a dim
star or the ghost of the last dandelion.
Alone in the vast warmth of her sleep,
she preserves in silence a royal Word
that will restart the world's stopped pulse and
call back that court the wind has blown away.

THOMAS R. SMITH

Ground Bees

In mid-day heat,
sparks leap about
a hole in the grass.

Two-way mystery,
the dark descent
and the rising into light,

two directions
the imagination
travels at once.

Practicality
recommends
a brutal remedy—

boiling water
or sand-fill to quench
that bright dance,

swarming frenzy
as of bits torn
from the flesh of the sun.

But I will ignore—
and not for the first time—
impoverished utility,

and delight in the luminous
industry of that unseen
forge in earth,

womb of myths,
foundry of stories,
striking from summer

dawn to summer dusk
seeds of living
fire into the world.

THOMAS R. SMITH

Bee-Catching

In a twenty-foot wilderness of weeds,
we caught honeybees. Wild prizes, they
fretted inside wide-mouthed glass jars,
under screw-on lids jackknifed with slits.
Sprawling or kneeling, we'd sneak up on some
worker gleaning a dandelion or purple thistle
and clap it prisoner, often as not
beheading the host flower in the name of our
hunt. Stinging was a constant possibility,
if not by a barbed behind then by nettles'
poison or thistles' daggers. Doggedly we'd
return, bactined and band-aided, to the game,
wonderful and risky, that bound us to
that tangled plot long into the summer
evening, determined not to go home
before the bees did. Sometimes it seemed
as though the weeds themselves held the sun
from setting. We kept a tight rein
on the earth, wound its green mane in our
fingers, took its green stain on our knees.
Even then we knew the complicated
pleasure of mixing danger and beauty,
the angry jewels we could capture
for a while, but which would drop, lusterless,
among clipped-off flowers if at the end
of the day we neglected to set the jar
in darkening grass, unscrew the lid, and run.

KIM STAFFORD

Nuptial Flight

The big buzz drone has been
in a holding pattern up
sixty feet, waiting for days.

The virgin queen, svelte
honey-skin ballerina,
rises to his station.

Coupled, tumbling, giving
her seed enough for a life
of labor, he shatters, debris.

Heavy, she descends
to the hive lip, limps in,
begins to lay a thousand

every day, single mother dipping
abdomen into cell after cell, while
all around her dance their children.

WILLIAM STAFFORD

A Memorial: Son Bret

In the way you went you were important.
I do not know what you found.
In the pattern of my life you stand
where you always stood, at the center,
a hero, a puzzle, a man.

What you might have told me
I will never know—the lips went still,
the body cold. I am afraid,
in the circling stars, in the dark,
and even at noon in the light.

When I run what am I running from?
You turned once to tell me something,
but then you glimpsed a shadow on my face
and maybe thought, Why tell what hurts?
You carried it, my boy, so brave, so far.

Now we have all the days, and the sun
goes by the same: there is a faint,
wandering trail I find sometimes, off
through grass and sage. I stop
and listen: only summer again—remember?—

The bees, the wind.

PAULINE STAINER

The Honeycomb

They had made love early in the high bed,
Not knowing the honeycomb stretched
Between lath and plaster of the outer wall.

For a century
The bees had wintered there,
Prisoning sugar in the virgin wax.

At times of transition,
Spring and autumn,
Their vibration swelled the room.

Laying his hands against the plaster
In the May sunrise,
He felt the faint frequency of their arousal,

Nor winters later, burning the beeswax candle,
Could he forget his tremulous first loving
Into the humming dawn.

ANNE STEVENSON

The Miracle of the Bees and the Foxgloves

Because hairs on their speckled daybeds baffle the little bees,
foxgloves hang their shingles out for rich bumbling hummers,
who crawl into their tunnels-of-delight with drunken ease
(see Darwin's pages on his foxglove summers)
plunging over heckles caked with sex-appealing stuff,
to sip from every hooker its intoxicating liquor
that stops it propagating in a corner with itself.

And this is how the foxglove keeps its sex life in order.
Two anthers—adolescent, in a hurry to dehisce—
let fly too soon, so pollen lies in drifts about the floor.
Along swims bumbler bee and makes an undercoat of this,
reverses, exits, lets it fall by accident next door.
So ripeness climbs the bells of *Digitalis* flower by flower,
undistracted by a Mind, or a Design, or by desire.

JOYCE SUTPHEN

Straight out of View

I'm thinking of birds—not only white ones.
I'm thinking of all the birds in the *Golden Book of Birds,*
and of their nests, and the parts of the country
where they're likely to be found.

Tepees and moonlight,
I'm thinking of owls and winter roads,
of quiet smoke ascending,
twisting out of the skin cone.
Shadows, rocking against the fire.

Chamomile and honey bees,
netted masks, and keeper's gloves.
Queens and drones and mysterious
dancing under the basswood leaves.
I'm thinking these wooden boxes,
the smooth-jointed edges of the hive,
are grayed like no other coffin.

Three-legged dogs and marshes,
tall reedy places where blackbirds wing.
Flaming eyes in the hillside,
the dragon kiln stoked and breathing fire.
A black kiss smothers the clay.

I'm thinking of ink,
letters fading,
and words that are fragile.
They begin to fly away as birds do:
suddenly, straight out of view.

BARTON SUTTER

The Visitor

The man whose muscles I once admired
Answers my knock with a vague smile,
Sure I'm a stranger who's made a mistake.
My name brings a laugh and a handshake.
He draws me in, calling his wife to the kitchen.
Mary, once mysterious and thin,
Has thickened. And John, the man
Whose boys would hightail it home
Like a pair of buckshot pups
When he whistled them to supper,
This man's giving way to gravity.
He slumps. He's gray.
I like him even more than I did then.
A jug of honey heats on the stove,
The crystals turning to liquid amber,
While the coffeepot mutters
And we discuss the Andersons' daughter,
Who died of what and who
Gave up and why they moved,
Which old bat had it coming,
Who went to jail, who made a killing,
Who loved who and had a bastard,
Small-town triumphs, personal disasters.

And after the coffee and strawberries,
I say my goodbyes to Mary
And troll the large lawn with John,
Fishing for memories and finding these
Fruits of his faith: two maple trees,
Willowy and weak when we were young,

Casting astonishing clouds of shade.
I imagine autumn, see red,
And we talk of his apples and cherries.
I tell him how many young people
Would envy the place that he's made.
He's proud, but he says that it's simple.
"Just plant and stay put. Things grow."
Myself, I can dream up a harvest
And even imagine a moment in winter, with frost
Like a frieze on the windows,
When you're snug and sit back and smile
At the red-and-white bite in the apple.
But where do you get the patience, the faith?
My life's more like water than trees.
We inspect his boxes of bees,
And the air grows thick with the hum
Of the engine of work and belief.

I have to run. John hands me a gift
Through the window. I hit the gas
And I'm gone. The town belongs to Mary and John
And the friendly strangers who wave as I pass.
I see that old abandoned place
The Nelsons rebuilt is abandoned again.
The engine drones. I shift and slow
For the curve that threw
A carload of kids twenty years ago.
I feel the same centrifugal tug,
But I'm out of the curve and over the hill,
The landscape reeling while the car stands still.
I steady the needle at sixty
And glance at the gift on the carseat
Beside me: a glowing hunk of honeycomb
The bees in their language of legs called home.
Tonight, in my room in the city,
I will sample those delicate spaces
And imagine other lives, other places.

BARTON SUTTER

Haiku

BIG WIND

The wind gave the trees
Such a thrashing I felt
Sorry for the bees.

MAY SWENSON

A Couple

A bee rolls in the yellow rose.
Does she invite his hairy rub?
He scrubs himself in her creamy folds . . . .
When he's done his honey-thieving
at her matrix, whirs free, leaving,
she closes, still tall, chill,
unrumpled on her stem.

Entrances and Exits

In the late afternoon, my friend's daughter walks into my office looking for snacks. She opens the bottom file drawer to take out a bag of rice cakes and a blue carton of rice milk that comes with its own straw. I have been looking at a book of paintings by Duccio. Olivia eats. Bits of puffed rice fall to the carpet.

A few hours ago, the 76-year-old woman, missing for two weeks in the wilderness, was found alive at the bottom of a canyon. The men who found her credit ravens. They noticed ravens circling—

Duccio's *Annunciation* sits open on my desk. The slender angel (dark, green-tipped wings folded behind him) reaches his right hand towards the girl; a vase of lilies sits behind them. But the white dots above the vase don't look like lilies. They look like the bits of puffed rice scattered under my desk. They look like the white fleck at the top of the painting that means both spirit and bird.

Olivia, who is six, picks up the wooden kaleidoscope from my desk and, holding it to her eye, turns it to watch the patterns honeycomb, the colors tumble and change—

Today is the 6th of September. In six days, Russia will hold a day of conception: couples will be given time off from work to procreate, and those who give birth on Russia's national day will receive money, cars, refrigerators, and other prizes.

A six hour drive from where I sit, deep in the Wallowa Mountains, the woman spent at least six days drifting in and out of consciousness, listening to the swellings of wind, the howls of coyotes, the shaggy-throated ravens—

I turn on the radio. Because he died this morning, Pavarotti's immoderate, unnatural Cs ring out. He said that, singing these notes, he was seized by an animal sensation so intense he would almost lose consciousness.

Duccio's subject is God's entrance into time: time meaning history, meaning a body.

No one knows how the woman survived in her light clothes, what she ate and drank, or what she thought when she looked up into the unkindness of ravens, their loops, their green and purple iridescence flashing—

I think of honeybees. For months, whole colonies have been disappearing from their hives. Where are the bodies? Some blame droughts. Too few flowers, they say: too little nectar.

Consider the ravens. They neither sow nor reap, they have neither storehouse nor barn, and yet God feeds them. (Luke 12:24)

The men never saw the ravens—just heard their deep *caw, caw* circling.

Olivia and I look down on Duccio's scene. I point to the angel's closed lips; she points to his dark wings.

The blue container of rice milk fits loosely into Olivia's hand the same way the book fits into the hand of Duccio's Mary. She punches a hole in the top and, until it is empty, Olivia drinks.

ALFRED LORD TENNYSON

Come Down, O Maid

Come down, O maid, from yonder mountain height:
What pleasure lives in height (the shepherd sang),
In height and cold, the splendour of the hills?
But cease to move so near the Heavens, and cease
To glide a sunbeam by the blasted Pine,
To sit a star upon the sparkling spire;
And come, for Love is of the valley, come,
For Love is of the valley, come thou down
And find him; by the happy threshold, he,
Or hand in hand with Plenty in the maize,
Or red with spirted purple of the vats,
Or foxlike in the vine; nor cares to walk
With Death and Morning on the silver horns,
Nor wilt thou snare him in the white ravine,
Nor find him dropt upon the firths of ice,
That huddling slant in furrow-cloven falls
To roll the torrent out of dusky doors:
But follow; let the torrent dance thee down
To find him in the valley; let the wild
Lean-headed Eagles yelp alone, and leave
The monstrous ledges there to slope, and spill
Their thousand wreaths of dangling water-smoke,
That like a broken purpose waste in air:
So waste not thou; but come; for all the vales
Await thee; azure pillars of the hearth
Arise to thee; the children call, and I
Thy shepherd pipe, and sweet is every sound,

Sweeter thy voice, but every sound is sweet;
Myriads of rivulets hurrying thro' the lawn,
The moan of doves in immemorial elms,
And murmuring of innumerable bees.

MAURICE THOMPSON

Wild Honey

I

Where hints of racy sap and gum
Out of the old dark forest come;

Where birds their beaks like hammers wield,
And pith is pierced and bark is peeled;

Where the green walnut's outer rind
Gives precious bitterness to the wind,—

There lurks the sweet creative power,
As lurks the honey in the flower.

II

A subtile effluence floats around
Where sheathèd shootlets break the ground;

And in each blossom's magic cup,
From infinite deeps a thought comes up.

III

In winter's bud that bursts in spring,
In nut of autumn's ripening,

In acrid bulb beneath the mould,
Sleeps the elixir, strong and old,

That Rosicrucians sought in vain,—
Life that renews itself again!

IV

What bottled perfume is so good
As fragrance of split tulip-wood?

What fabled drink of god or muse
Was rich as purple mulberry-juice?

And what school-polished gem of thought
Is like the rune from Nature caught?

V

He is a poet strong and true
Who loves wild thyme and honey-dew;

And like a brown bee works and sings
With morning freshness on his wings,

And a golden burden on his thighs,—
The pollen-dust of centuries!

JEANIE TOMASKO

Sweetness

God gave the honeybee six weeks
and so
she flies
five hundred miles
in short refrains
of alleluias
to windy, white clover fields
to pink and proper rose gardens
gathering nectar in that careful needle
taking no time for self-pity, though
her life's work, together
with that of eleven sisters
was the teaspoon of honey
I just stirred into my tea.

Sometimes she stops to walk
on my sunflowers,
her sturdy legs grow heavy
as she fills her pollen-baskets
with food for the bees back home,
but I like to think her stroll
on those upturned yellow faces
is more for the joy of making me wonder
what I know of happiness.

JEANIE TOMASKO

Watching Bees

Knowing you were tired of death
we spoke of other things,
traded stories
about our fathers,
dogs we used to have,
your trip to Paris—how you
bargained with the artist
for the painting of the woman
with your sister's eyes.
We watched the afternoon light
play on the table, the color
of saffron, you said,
and you wished
for energy to dust the dust.

And now I'm watching bees
on a Saturday morning, hovering
around the fading violet
hosta flowers—and you
are back in the hospital.

We were like bees
that day—skimming what was left
of the late-summer air,
entering small doorways,
rummaging like thieves
for any last sweetness.

JEAN VALENTINE

Bees

—FOR SANDRA MCPHERSON

A man whose arms and shoulders
and hands and face and ears are covered with bees
says, *I've never known such pain.*
Another man comes over
with bees all over his hands—
only bees can get the other bees off.
The first man says again,
I've never known such pain.
The second man's bees begin to pluck
the first grave yellow bees off, one by one.

The Nature and Qualities of Bees

Come now and I'll impart the qualities Jupiter himself
gave bees, for which reward they followed after
the melodious sounds and clashing bronze of the Curetes,
and fed Heaven's king in the Dictean cave.
They alone hold children in common: own the roofs
of their city as one: and pass their life under the might of the law.
They alone know a country, and a settled home,
and in summer, remembering the winter to come,
undergo labour, storing their gains for all.
For some supervise the gathering of food, and work
in the fields to an agreed rule: some, walled in their homes,
lay the first foundations of the comb, with drops of gum
taken from narcissi, and sticky glue from tree-bark,
then hang the clinging wax: others lead the mature young,
their nation's hope, others pack purest honey together,
and swell the cells with liquid nectar:
there are those whose lot is to guard the gates,
and in turn they watch out for rain and clouds in the sky,
or accept the incoming loads, or, forming ranks,
they keep the idle crowd of drones away from the hive.
The work glows, and the fragrant honey is sweet with thyme.
And like the Cyclopes when they forge lightning bolts
quickly, from tough ore, and some make the air come and go
with ox-hide bellows, others dip hissing bronze
in the water: Etna groans with the anvils set on her:
and they lift their arms together with great and measured force,
and turn the metal with tenacious tongs:
so, if we may compare small things with great,
an innate love of creation spurs the Attic bees on,

each in its own way. The older ones take care of the hive,
and building the comb, and the cleverly fashioned cells.
But at night the weary young carry back sacs filled with thyme:
they graze far and wide on the blossom of strawberry-trees,
and pale-grey willows, and rosemary and bright saffron,
on rich lime-trees and on purple hyacinths.
All have one rest from work: all have one labour:
they rush from the gates at dawn: no delay: when the evening star
has warned them to leave their grazing in the fields again,
then they seek the hive, then they refresh their bodies:
there's a buzzing, a hum around the entrances and thresholds.
Then when they've settled to rest in their cells, there's silence
in the night, and sleep seizes their weary limbs.
If rain's threatening they don't go far from their hives,
or trust the sky when Easterlies are nearing,
but fetch water from nearby, in the safety of their city wall,
and try brief flights, and often lift little stones,
as unstable ships take up ballast in a choppy sea,
and balance themselves with these in the vaporous clouds.
And you'll wonder at this habit that pleases the bees,
that they don't indulge in sexual union, or lazily relax
their bodies in love, or produce young in labour,
but collect their children in their mouths themselves from leaves,
and sweet herbs, provide a new leader and tiny citizens
        themselves,
and remake their palaces and waxen kingdoms.
Often too as they wander among harsh flints they bruise
their wings, and breathe their lives away beneath their burden,
so great is their love of flowers, and glory in creating honey.
And though the end of a brief life awaits the bees themselves
(since it never extends beyond the seventh summer)
the species remains immortal, and the fortune of the hive
is good for many years, and grandfathers' grandfathers are
        counted.
Besides, Egypt and mighty Lydia and the Parthian tribes,

and the Median Hydaspes do not pay such homage to their leader.
With the leader safe all are of the same mind:
if the leader's lost they break faith, and tear down the honey
they've made, themselves, and dissolve the latticed combs.
The leader is the guardian of their labours: to the leader
they do reverence, and all sit round the leader in a noisy throng,
and crowd round in large numbers, and often
they lift the leader on their shoulders and expose their bodies
in war, and, among wounds, seek a glorious death.
Noting these tokens and examples some have said
that a share of divine intelligence is in bees,
and a draught of *aether*: since there is a god in everything,
earth and the expanse of sea and the sky's depths:
from this source the flocks and herds, men, and every species
of creature, each derive their little life, at birth:
to it surely all then return, and dissolved, are remade,
and there is no room for death, but still living
they fly to the ranks of the stars, and climb the high heavens.

—*from* The Georgics, *Book IV, 149–227*
(*translated by A. S. Kline*)

ELLEN BRYANT VOIGT

The Farmer

In the still-blistering late afternoon,
like currying a horse the rake
circled the meadow, the cut grass ridging
behind it. This summer, if the weather held,
he'd risk a second harvest after years
of reinvesting, leaving fallow.
These fields were why he farmed—
he walked the fenceline like a man in love.
The animals were merely what he needed:
cattle and pigs; chickens for awhile; a drayhorse,
saddle horses he was paid to pasture—
an endless stupid round
of animals, one of them was always hungry, sick, lost,
calving or farrowing, or waiting slaughter.

When the field began dissolving in the dusk,
he carried feed down to the knoll,
its clump of pines, gate, trough, lick, chute
and two gray hives; leaned into the Jersey's side
as the galvanized bucket filled with milk;
released the cow and turned to the bees.
He'd taken honey before without protection.

This time, they could smell something
in his sweat—fatigue? impatience,
although he was a stubborn, patient man?
Suddenly, like flame, they were swarming over him.

He rolled in the dirt, manure and stiff hoof-prints,
started back up the path, rolled in the fresh hay—

refused to run, which would have pumped
the venom through him faster—passed the oaks
at the yard's edge, rolled in the yard, reached
the kitchen, and when he tore off his clothes
crushed bees dropped from him like scabs.

For a week he lay in the darkened bedroom.
The doctor stopped by twice a day—
the hundred stings "enough to kill an ox,
enough to kill a younger man." What saved him
were the years of smaller doses—
like minor disappointments,
instructive poison, something he could use.

G. C. WALDREP

Their Faces Shall Be As Flames

That was the spring the bees disappeared, we didn't know
    where they went, where they'd gone, where they were going,
        it was a
rapture of the bees, only the weak, the young, the freshly dead
left behind, *a rapture of bees,* my neighbor with the ducks had
        begun to walk
like a duck, *Follow follow follow Sam* he sang as he walked, and
        they followed
it was that simple, of course I thought of the Piper, although
this procession was more benign, my neighbor's I mean, though
        he intended
to have each for dinner, eventually, and he did not name them,
as we don't name bees, because we don't see clearly enough
to distinguish them as persons, *person* in the grammatical sense,
        first second
or third, which is why we refer to them in the collective, usually,
they breed, they swarm, they milk their honey for us
in the collective, and they vanish collectively, is this then the true
rapture, was the one true God after all a god of bees, and now
        she is taking
them home, is this any more comforting than all the other
        proposed explanations,
pesticide, fungus, mites, electromagnetism, even the infrasound
        the giant
windmills make, that sends the bats and raptors
to their deaths, all invention gone awry, hive after hive
suddenly empty, as if they'd all flown out less than purposefully,
        casually,
and somehow forgotten to come back, held up at the doctor's
        or the U-Haul

dealer's, swarms of them, hundreds, thousands vagabond
in some other landscape, or rising, *we shall meet them in the air,*
at the post office to mail a letter to a woman who might or might
        not be my love
because a rate change had caught me with insufficient postage
I had to wait, the clerk was preoccupied with a sort of crate
made of wire mesh, through which I could see bees, *Resistant*
        the clerk said
as she filled out the forms and sent them, registered parcel post,
        somewhere
else, only then did she sell me the stamp I needed,
or thought I needed, or hoped to need (there is a season
when one hopes to need), and I thought about what it would
        be like
to mail a crate of bees, *Resistant,* to my love, if I had a love,
        and have them
vanish en route, the mesh crate arriving dusty, empty, one or two
broken, desiccated bodies rattling lightly around inside, like seeds
        in a gourd,
or like a child you'll never have, that is, the possibility of that
        child, the rattling
blood of it, a different sort of vanishing, we would all like to
        believe
in the act, that Houdini was a man, only a man, as he proved in
        the moment
and by the precise circumstance of his death, and the fact of his
        body,
lifeless but extant, rattling around the arcade, the park, the
        amusement pier
of disturbing coincidences, while in Missouri another hobbyist
        beekeeper
walks out to her tomblike hives on a spring morning
to find nothing there, just boxes, empty boxes, a sort of game
a child might invent, this rapture, same sort of funny story
a child *will* invent, when shown a photograph, *This is the
        policeman,*

and this is the woman with two heads, and this, which looks like
  a modest
red house in a suburb, this is really the ghost of the bees,
a small ghost, a modest ghost, like the ghosts of the locusts
  and the elms,
not a ghost to trouble us, until (in the photograph) the house
  spreads its wings
and vanishes, as houses do, or as houses will when the rapture
  extends
to architecture, the god of small houses having, first, existed,
  and then wed
the bee god, so that we are left sleeping alone again, and out of
  doors, in spring,
as one more source of sweetness is subtracted from this world
and added to another, perhaps, as we would like to think,
  one of the
more comforting ideas, a sort of economics, a grand
accounting, until what angel of houses or of bees blows what
  trumpet,
and we fall as mountains upon the insects, devour them as seas,
scorch the houses as with fire, *we* become the ground that
  hollows beneath
them and the air they fly through, their wormwood star, as all
  the bees of heaven
watch from heaven and all the houses of heaven lean down
for a closer look, and the smoke drifts upward, and we are the
  smoke, we are
only the smoke, inside of which my neighbor walks, with his
  ducks, and sings,
and they follow, and my hive lazes, drowses as if they or it were
  dreaming
us, as if they or us were touchable, simple as a story, an
  explanation,
any fiction, as if they thought of us, or were praying, or were
  dancing,
or were lonely, as if they could be, or would be touched.

MICHAEL WALSH

Abandoned House with Vagrant Bees

They break into the walls,
and before long, the house hums
attic to floor. Windows

boarded, doors
barred, no one knows.
Workers pry dusty

sex from noxious
weeds, pet roses.
They raid neat-freak tulip

plots, bleak church beds
and big box garden lots.
The bee comb builds up,

ridged like mushrooms
inside rotting beams.
No one walking past, cell

phone in hand, knows
how much sunlight
hangs inside, curing.

CONNIE WANEK

Pollen

The neighbor's bees, his chattel,
are healthy again, and back they've come
to work in my garden.

What shelter's more felicitous than
a squash blossom? The bees are busy, yes,
but do they know enough to call that happiness?

Living dust clings to their legs
and wings. Six male flowers tremble
for every pregnant bloom,

and to touch them is a terrible intimacy.
How can bees be property?
How can a garden?

Small white houses in an orchard:
A good life, near the children,
near the graves.

J. P. WHITE

The Macadamia Nut Bees

One can argue all bees are happy
   or all bees in the field are too busy
plying their trade to be unhappy.
Like them, this is where we live,
inside the heated cage of pollen
between happy and unhappy.

Standing under a macadamia nut tree,
I peered into the upper hollow
and heard the essence
of the perpetual between,
the tree itself a strumming
of luminary strings of pink flowers.

So hard to crack, so rare to fall,
the macadamias swing
from long, green stems,
and remain cloaked and aloof
like treasures always do.
Not the macadamia bees.

They crawl and nuzzle
the soft, tendril lanterns
and make of April a clamoring
for more setting out and returning,
more music lingering between
honeyed kingdoms.

WALT WHITMAN

from "Spontaneous Me"

Earth of chaste love—life that is only life after love,
The body of my love—the body of the woman I love—the
body of the man—the body of the earth,
Soft forenoon airs that blow from the south-west,
The hairy wild-bee that murmurs and hankers up and down,
that gripes the
full-grown lady-flower, curves upon her with amorous firm legs,
takes
his will of her, and holds himself tremulous and tight till he is
satisfied,
The wet woods through the early hours,
Two sleepers at night lying close together as they sleep, one with
an arm slanted down
and across and below the waist of the other . . .

(lines 14–19)

JOHN GREENLEAF WHITTIER

Telling the Bees

Here is the place; right over the hill
Runs the path I took;
You can see the gap in the old wall still,
And the stepping-stones in the shallow brook.

There is the house, with the gate red-barred,
And the poplars tall;
And the barn's brown length, and the cattle-yard,
And the white horns tossing above the wall.

There are the beehives ranged in the sun;
And down by the brink
Of the brook are her poor flowers, weed-o'errun,
Pansy and daffodil, rose and pink.

A year has gone, as the tortoise goes,
Heavy and slow;
And the same rose blows, and the same sun glows,
And the same brook sings of a year ago.

There's the same sweet clover-smell in the breeze;
And the June sun warm
Tangles his wings of fire in the trees,
Setting, as then, over Fernside farm.

I mind me how with a lover's care
From my Sunday coat
I brushed off the burrs, and smoothed my hair,
And cooled at the brookside my brow and throat.

Since we parted, a month had passed,—
To love, a year;

191

Down through the beeches I looked at last
On the little red gate and the well-sweep near.

I can see it all now,—the slantwise rain
Of light through the leaves,
The sundown's blaze on her window-pane,
The bloom of her roses under the eaves.

Just the same as a month before,—
The house and the trees,
The barn's brown gable, the vine by the door,—
Nothing changed but the hives of bees.

Before them, under the garden wall,
Forward and back,
Went drearily singing the chore-girl small,
Draping each hive with a shred of black.

Trembling, I listened: the summer sun
Had the chill of snow;
For I knew she was telling the bees of one
Gone on the journey we all must go!

Then I said to myself, "My Mary weeps
For the dead to-day:
Haply her blind old grandsire sleeps
The fret and the pain of his age away."

But her dog whined low; on the doorway sill,
With his cane to his chin,
The old man sat; and the chore-girl still
Sung to the bees stealing out and in.

And the song she was singing ever since
In my ear sounds on:—
"Stay at home, pretty bees, fly not hence!
Mistress Mary is dead and gone!"

NANCY WILLARD

Bees Swarming

Just at noon in the summer I hear them.
  Behind the house the hives stare
like tombstones in the tall grass.
But a small hum rises in the air,

high hymns of women in a wooden church.
Their gathering swells in the long heat.
Now they hang on the air like a pouch of gold,
singers and sextons of the plum and wheat.

My grandfather covers himself with black,
eclipses himself in a net to his knees,
costume that cries, I am invisible,
the hooded hunter of the innocent bees.

The net in his hand leaps and the glaze of noise
contracts to a frantic ball.
Now I hear nothing but cries and lament,
bodies and wings as they fall.

"So it must be," says my grandfather,
doffing his net and his hood—he is not
a cruel man. "So it must be.
If they are to make the gold, they must be caught

and made to live in the dark hive.
That's where the apple and plum
change to mineral sweetness
and divisible sun."

NANCY WILLARD

The Poet Enters the Sleep of the Bees

Turning to honey one morning, I passed
through their glass cells and entered
the sleep of the bees.
The bees were making a lexicon
of the six-sided names of God,

clover's breath, dewflesh,
ritual of the thorn, a definitive work
to graft the names to their roots.
For days I hiked over their sleepshod sounds.
At last I saw a green lion
eating a hole in the sun,

and a red dragon burning itself alive
to melt the snow that lay like a cap
on the sleep of the bees.
Their sleep was a factory
of sweetness with no author.

Every syllable was swept clean,
every act was without motive.
Please forgive me this poor translation.
How could I hold
my past to my present when I heard
ten thousand tongues flowing along like gold?

MORGAN GRAYCE WILLOW

One Clover, and a Bee

—TO EMILY DICKINSON

I'd like to get my confidence back,
that sense of play while digging in the dirt,
the easy brushing away without fear
of those bothersome things, bees
in flight or creeping worms,
death, near at hand, yet having no sting.

No more. Not since that sting
one July afternoon laid me flat out on my back,
brought me face to face with the old worm,
death, its patient presence in the dirt.
The sudden discovery of an allergy to bees
opens gateways to unknown fears.

I used to flaunt other people's fear,
insist that bees never sting
if you just stay still, simply let them be.
Now I take it all back.
Before, I loved the garden's dirt.
Now, the black tunnel worms

its way into everything. Even earthworms,
welcome soil-builders, bring a tinge of fear
as I long to get my hands in dirt.
Gardening's become a song of death, sting,
and loss. No more bee balm planted out back
tempting wasps, yellow jackets, even honeybees.

My favorite poem refers to a bee.
I wear it on the back of my shirt. Bees worm
their way through many poems, a paying back
of dues, perhaps, not to be read with fear
in those lines. Yet now, even that stings
a bit, even words now treacherous as dirt.

It's hard to remove, persistent as dirt
under fingernails, the threat inside each bee.
I can't convince myself it won't sting,
that it's as necessary to the garden as worms.
Stored among rakes and hoes, now, is fear
which time won't reverse or take back.

Dirt to dust, ashes to ashes, the worm,
the bee, the newness of fear.
The sting. I want my equilibrium back.

ELEANOR RAND WILNER

The Girl with Bees in Her Hair

came in an envelope with no return address;
she was small, wore a wrinkled dress of figured
cotton, full from neck to ankles, with a button
of bone at the throat, a collar of torn lace.
She was standing before a monumental house—
on the scale you see in certain English films:
urns, curved drives, stone lions, and an entrance far
too vast for any home. She was not of that place,
for she had a foreign look, and tangled black hair,
and an ikon, heavy and strange, dangling from
an oversize chain around her neck, that looked
as if some tall adult had taken it from his,
and hung it there as a charm to keep her safe
from a world of infinite harm that soon
would take him far from her, and leave her
standing, as she stood now—barefoot, gazing
without expression into distance, away
from the grandeur of that house, its gravel
walks and sculpted gardens. She carried a basket
full of flames, but whether fire or flowers
with crimson petals shading toward a central gold,
was hard to say—though certainly, it burned,
and the light within it had nowhere else
to go, and so fed on itself, intensified its red
and burning glow, the only color in the scene.
The rest was done in grays, light and shadow
as they played along her dress, across her face,
and through her midnight hair, lively with bees.
At first they seemed just errant bits of shade,

until the humming grew too loud to be denied
as the bees flew in and out, as if choreographed
in a country dance between the fields of sun
and the black tangle of her hair.
Without warning
a window on one of the upper floors flew open—
wind had caught the casement, a silken length
of curtain filled like a billowing sail—the bees
began to stream out from her hair, straight
to the single opening in the high facade. Inside,
a moment later—the sound of screams.

The girl—who had through all of this seemed
unconcerned and blank—all at once looked up.
She shook her head, her mane of hair freed
of its burden of bees, and walked away,
out of the picture frame, far beyond
the confines of the envelope that brought her
image here—here, where the days grow longer
now, the air begins to warm, dread grows to
fear among us, and the bees swarm.

JAMES WRIGHT

The First Days

OPTIMA DIES PRIMA FUGIT

The first thing I saw in the morning
Was a huge golden bee ploughing
His burly right shoulder into the belly
Of a sleek yellow pear
Low on a bough.
Before he could find the sudden black honey
That squirms around in there
Inside the seed, the tree could not bear any more.
The pear fell to the ground,
With the bee still half alive
Inside its body.
He would have died if I hadn't knelt down
And sliced the pear gently
A little more open.
The bee shuddered, and returned.
Maybe I should have left him alone there,
Drowning in his own delight.
The best days are the first
To flee, sang the lovely
Musician born in this town
So like my own.
I let the bee go
Among the gasworks at the edge of Mantua.

WILLIAM BUTLER YEATS

The Lake Isle of Innisfree

I will arise and go now, and go to Innisfree,
  And a small cabin build there of clay and wattles made;
Nine bean-rows will I have there, a hive for the honeybee,
And live alone in the bee-loud glade.

And I shall have some peace there, for peace comes dropping
    slow,
Dropping from the veils of the morning to where the cricket
    sings;
There midnight's all a glimmer, and noon a purple glow,
And evening full of the linnet's wings.

I will arise and go now, for always night and day
I hear lake water lapping with low sounds by the shore;
While I stand on the roadway, or on the pavements grey,
I hear it in the deep heart's core.

from "Meditations in Time of Civil War"

VI. THE STARE'S NEST BY MY WINDOW

The bees build in the crevices
Of loosening masonry, and there
The mother birds bring grubs and flies.
My wall is loosening; honey-bees,
Come build in the empty house of the stare.

We are closed in, and the key is turned
On our uncertainty; somewhere
A man is killed, or a house burned,
Yet no clear fact to be discerned:
Come build in the empty house of the stare.

A barricade of stone or of wood;
Some fourteen days of civil war;
Last night they trundled down the road
That dead young soldier in his blood:
Come build in the empty house of the stare.

We had fed the heart on fantasies,
The heart's grown brutal from the fare;
More Substance in our enmities
Than in our love; O honey-bees,
Come build in the empty house of the stare.

Note: "stare" is starling in the west of Ireland, according to Yeats.

TIMOTHY YOUNG

The Bee and the Mosquito

Honeybees prefer the nectar
of the youngest blossoms.

Ground bees delight in
ripened fruit on the grass.

The honeybee turns nectar to honey,
then dies and is pushed from the hive.

The ground bee dies sated
in the sugar of fallen fruit.

Marla Spivak

Every day I strive to see the world from the bees' point of view. I have to. The questions I pose to bees through scientific inquiry, and the answers they give me, require this shift in perception. My beekeeping skills and my ability to teach others about bees depend on pushing perception beyond the human horizon and into the heart and realm of the bee super-organism. To understand bees, I need to think like a bee.

> We are bees,
> and our body is a honeycomb.
> We made
> the body, cell by cell we made it.
> —*Jelaluddin Rumi*

I try to avoid ambiguity, symbolism, and irony when I have my head in a beehive. Nor do I spend my days thinking about bees rhythmically or musically. But Alfred Lord Tennyson wrote an incredible four words—"murmuring of innumerable bees"— that captures lectures on lectures of bee biology.

When a bee colony is happy and healthy, it radiates. The aroma from a healthy hive (the mixture of flowers, beeswax, propolis, and bees) is like nothing else on earth. Pablo Neruda knew this: "I will never forget their fragrance."

When a bee colony is not well, it sounds off-key, looks frowsy, and smells of decay. More and more these days, bee colonies are not well. Sick bees hold a mirror that puts humans into sharp focus. Our landscaping practices have turned many agricultural and urban areas into flowerless, toxic wastelands. We have made it hard for the bumblebee to exalt . . .

Extraordinary
The simple white rose
Of the thimbleberry.
—Barton Sutter

. . . because the berry may be contaminated with an insecticide, or not even present in the landscape because it was paved over, plowed under, or burned off by herbicides. What would our world be like without bees?

No more apples to bite into for knowledge,
Their silence will sting our throats closed.
—Susan Deborah King

the flowers, unkindled
will blaze
one last time
and go out
—Linda Pastan

Reading these poems, written across the ages, reinforces to me the power of bees to connect us to nature and to our hearts. We can help bees; it is relatively easy. Emily Dickinson knew the secret years ago:

To make a prairie, it takes a clover and one bee . . .

Please help our bees. Plant flowers, and keep those flowers free from pesticide contamination. When we nourish bees, we nourish ourselves. The collector of these poems, James P. Lenfestey, may have put it best:

Honey is food, the way poetry is food . . .

The bees and I thank you.

Contributors

SHERMAN ALEXIE is a poet, writer, and filmmaker. His writing often draws on his experiences as a Native American with ancestry of several tribes, growing up on the Spokane Indian Reservation. He lives in Seattle, Washington.

MAUREEN ASH keeps bees and bakes on a farm near River Falls, Wisconsin.

THORSTEN BACON is a Minnesota native now living in Michigan. He works as a jeweler.

ALIKI BARNSTONE is a poet, translator, and critic. She is a professor of English at the University of Missouri. Her most recent collection of poetry is *Bright Body,* and she is also author of *Dear God, Dear Dr. Heartbreak* and *Blue Earth,* among other books.

WILLIS BARNSTONE is an American poet, memoirist, translator, and a New Testament and Gnostic scholar. He has translated the Ancient Greek poets and the complete fragments of the philosopher Heraclitus.

JOHN BARR has published several books of poetry, including *The Hundred Fathom Curve* (expanded and updated as *The Hundred Fathom Curve: New and Collected Poems*) and the mock-epic *Grace: Book One of The Adventures of Ibn Opcit* and *Opcit at Large: Book Two of The Adventures of Ibn Opcit.* He lives in New York and Chicago.

TREE BERNSTEIN designs and edits books for TreeHouse Press. With Randy Roark, she has cowritten *Away,* a series of ghazals. She produces K–12 workshops with CPITS and is a poetry coach for Poetry Out Loud, a national recitation project.

BARRY BLUMENFELD lives in Minnesota. He is the author of the novel *O, Sinners*. "Barry Blumenfeld" is the pen name of Barry Brent.

ROBERT BLY is the internationally celebrated author of many books of poems, translations, and essays. His recent books include *Reaching Out to the World: Prose Poems* and *Stealing Sugar from the Castle: New and Selected Poems*. He lives in Minneapolis.

SEAN BORODALE is Creative Fellow at Trinity College, Cambridge University, England. He has published two collections of poetry: *Human Work (a poet's cookbook)* and *Bee Journal*, which was shortlisted for the T. S. Eliot Prize and the Costa Book Award.

KARINA BOROWICZ is a poet and a translator from Russian and French.

LAURE-ANNE BOSSELAAR is a native of Belgium. She is the author of *The Hour Between Dog and Wolf*, *Small Gods of Grief*, which won the Isabella Gardner Prize for Poetry, and *A New Hunger*, selected as Notable Book 2008 by the American Library Association.

JILL BRECKENRIDGE has been awarded a Bush Foundation Fellowship, two State Arts Board Grants, and Loft–McKnight Writers' Awards in poetry and creative prose. Her books include *The Gravity of Flesh* and *Miss Priss and the Con Man*, a memoir.

FLEDA BROWN is professor emerita of English at the University of Delaware, where she founded the Poets in the Schools program. Her sixth collection of poems, *Reunion*, was awarded the Felix Pollak Prize in Poetry from the University of Wisconsin. She has coedited two books, most recently *On the Mason–Dixon Line: An Anthology of Contemporary Delaware Writers*.

ROBERT BURNS (1759–1796), a poet and lyricist writing in Scots as well as English, is the great national poet of Scotland.

JOHN BURNSIDE is a Scottish writer. His books of poetry have won the Whitbread Poetry Award, the Geoffrey Faber Memorial Prize, the Forward Prize, and the T. S. Eliot Prize. He lives in Fife, Scotland, and teaches at the University of St. Andrews. The poem series *Melissographia* is a limited-edition collaboration with artist Amy Shelton.

JOHN CADDY is a poet-naturalist who lives near Forest Lake, Minnesota. He has published poetry and books on arts education, and he writes the blog *Morning Earth* (www.morning -earth.org).

JARED CARTER lives in Indianapolis. Much of his early work is set in "Mississinewa County," an imaginary place that includes the actual Mississinewa River, a tributary of the Wabash River. His first collection of poetry, *Work, for the Night Is Coming,* won the Walt Whitman Award.

SHARON CHMIELARZ lives in Minneapolis. She has published seven books of poetry, including *The Other Mozart,* about the composer's sister, Nannerl. Her most recent collection is *Visibility: Ten Miles,* created with photographer Ken Smith.

LUCILLE CLIFTON (1936–2010) was an American poet, writer, and educator from Buffalo, New York. Her poetry often celebrates her African American heritage, women's experience, and the female body. Her books include *Mercy, Voices,* and *Blessing the Boats: New and Collected Poems.*

SAMUEL TAYLOR COLERIDGE (1772–1834), a poet, literary critic, and philosopher, was a founder of the English Romantic movement.

LORNA CROZIER was born in Swift Current, Saskatchewan. She has written fourteen books of poetry, including *The Garden Going on without Us, Angels of Flesh, Angels of Silence, Inventing the Hawk* (winner of the 1992 Governor-General's Award), *Everything Arrives at the Light, What the Living Won't Let Go,* and *Whetstone.*

ANNIE DEPPE teaches poetry at Eastern Connecticut State University. She is the author of *Sitting in the Sky*.

EMILY DICKINSON (1830–1886) is one of the most important and prolific American poets. Although fewer than a dozen of her poems were published during her lifetime, she is now among the most widely read poets. She lived in Amherst, Massachusetts.

JOSEPHINE DICKINSON, English poet and sheep farmer, is the author of *Scarberry Hill, The Voice,* and *Silence Fell*.

CAROL ANN DUFFY is a Scottish poet and playwright. She is professor of contemporary poetry at Manchester Metropolitan University and was appointed Britain's poet laureate in 2009. She has written many books of poems, including *The Bees*.

RALPH WALDO EMERSON (1803–1882) was a founder of the American Transcendentalist movement and was famous in his time for his speeches, poems, and luminous essays.

HEID E. ERDRICH is a vegetarian granddaughter of butchers. In 2009 she won the Minnesota Book Award for her poetry collection *National Monuments*.

EARL OF ESSEX (ROBERT DEVEREUX) (1565–1601) was an English aristocrat famed for his poetry, some of which was set to music in the sixteenth century by the composer John Dowland.

JOHN EVANS (1756–1846) was a Welsh surgeon. His interests included cartography and bees, and he wrote a didactic poem called "The Bee."

DIANE FAHEY is the author of twelve poetry collections, most recently *The Stone Garden: Poems from Clare,* shortlisted for the Kenneth Slessor Poetry Prize.

LAWRENCE FERLINGHETTI is a poet, proprietor of City Lights bookstore in San Francisco, and publisher of City Lights

Books. A seminal figure in the American Beat literary movement, his many books of poetry include the million-selling *A Coney Island of the Mind* and most recently *Time of Useful Consciousness (Americus Book II)*.

NICK FLYNN is the author of three collections of poetry, including *Some Ether,* which won the inaugural PEN/Joyce Osterweil Award for Poetry in 1999 and was a finalist for the Los Angeles Times Book Prize. His memoir, *Another Bullshit Night in Suck City,* was adapted into a film.

STUART FRIEBERT has published thirteen books of poems (among them *Funeral Pie,* cowinner of the Four Way Book Award), ten volumes of translations, and several anthologies (including *The Longman Anthology of Contemporary American Poetry,* coedited with David Young). With colleagues, he cofounded the writing program at Oberlin College, along with *Field* magazine, Oberlin College Press, and the Field Translation Series.

ROSS GAY's poems have been published in anthologies, literary journals, and magazines, including *American Poetry Review, Harvard Review, Columbia: A Journal of Poetry and Art, Margie: The American Journal of Poetry,* and *Atlanta Review.* He has been a Cave Canem Workshop fellow and a Bread Loaf Writers Conference Tuition Scholar.

EAMON GRENNAN is an Irish poet. Born in Dublin, he has lived in the United States, except for brief periods, since 1964. He was the Dexter M. Ferry Jr. Professor of English at Vassar College until his retirement in 2004. His collection *Out of Breath* was nominated for the 2008 Poetry Now Award.

BARBARA HAMBY is the author of *Eating Bees* and recipient of two Florida Arts Council fellowships, one in poetry and one in fiction. Her collection *Delirium* won the Vassar Miller Prize in Poetry.

TOM HENNEN grew up in western Minnesota and worked for wildlife agencies in Minnesota and South Dakota. During the 1970s, he was printer for the Minnesota Writers Publishing House. He has written the poetry collection *Darkness Sticks to Everything*.

JIM HEYNEN, poet and writer, is best known for his collections of short prose featuring young farm boys, including *The One-Room Schoolhouse: Stories about the Boys* and *The Man Who Kept Cigars in His Cap*. His most recent collection is *Ordinary Sins*.

SELIMA HILL is a British poet who grew up in rural England and Wales and now lives in Lyme Regis. Her most recent book of poetry is *People Who Like Meatballs*, which was shortlisted for the Forward Poetry Prize's Best Poetry Collection of the Year.

BRENDA HILLMAN is a California poet and environmental activist. Her books of poems include *Bright Existence*, *Cascadia*, and her most recent collection, *Seasonal Works with Letters on Fire*. She is the Olivia Filippi Professor of Poetry at Saint Mary's College in Moraga, California.

JANE HIRSHFIELD lives in Mill Valley, California. Her seven poetry books include *Come, Thief* and *After*. She has also written the essay collection *Nine Gates: Entering the Mind of Poetry*.

KEVIN HOLDEN is mostly from Rhode Island and now lives mostly in Connecticut. He is an activist and amateur geometer, and he cares a great deal about trees. His first book of poetry, *Solar*, is forthcoming in the Fence Modern Poets Series.

KOBAYASHI ISSA (1763–1828) is one of the classic Japanese haiku poets and a beloved poet of insects and frogs.

HELEN HUNT JACKSON (1830–1885) was a poet, novelist, and pioneering advocate for American Indians in her book *A Century of Dishonor*, published in 1881. She was a friend of Emily Dickinson.

NAOMI JACKSON recently retired as membership coordinator at Hampden Park Co-op in St. Paul, Minnesota. She has degrees in anthropology and theology. She is passionate about finding ways for humans to live more gently on the earth, and she seeks to connect with the rest of earth's creatures through beekeeping, poetry, gardening, and simple living.

GEORGE BENSON JOHNSTON (1913–2004) was a Canadian poet. He published as George Johnston and was best known for poetry that addressed suburban family life with humor and wisdom. He was a renowned scholar and translator of the Icelandic Sagas.

SUSAN DEBORAH KING has published several books of poetry, including *Tabernacle, Coven,* and, most recently, *One Life, One Meeting.* She lived for many years in Minnesota but recently moved to Maine.

RUDYARD KIPLING (1865–1936) was an English poet and novelist best known for his books *The Jungle Book* and *Kim.* He was among the most popular writers in Britain during the late nineteenth and early twentieth centuries.

D. H. LAWRENCE (1885–1930) was a poet and novelist. He wrote many poems about the natural world.

DAVID LEE has raised hogs, worked in a cotton mill, earned a Ph.D. with a specialty in the poetry of John Milton, and recently retired from the Department of Language and Literature at Southern Utah University. He was named Utah's first poet laureate and one of Utah's top twelve writers of all time by the Utah Endowment for the Humanities. He has been honored with grants from the National Endowment for the Arts.

JAMES P. LENFESTEY is a poet and journalist based in Minneapolis. He has written a book of personal essays and five collections of poetry, including *A Cartload of Scrolls: One Hundred Poems in the Manner of Han-shan* and *Into the Goodhue County Jail: Poems to Free Prisoners.* His haibun memoir, *Seeking the Cave,* was a finalist for the Minnesota Book Awards.

NATHANIEL "MAX" LENFESTEY is a poet, songwriter, and environmentalist living in Aptos, California.

DIANE LOCKWARD is the author of three poetry books, most recently *Temptation by Water*. Her book *What Feeds Us* received the 2006 Quentin R. Howard Poetry Prize. She has also written two chapbooks, *Against Perfection* and *Greatest Hits, 1997–2010*.

ANTONIO MACHADO (1875–1939) was one of the greatest Spanish poets of the twentieth century.

BRUCE MACKINNON teaches creative writing at The George Washington University in Washington, D.C. His *Mystery Schools* won the Washington Writers' Publishing House Prize in Poetry in 2007, and he was selected by Tom Sleigh as an Academy of American Poets Prize winner.

OSIP MANDELSTAM (1891–1938) was an influential Russian modernist poet. After publishing a poem that mocked Stalin, he was sent to a gulag, where he died.

THOMAS MCCARTHY is an Irish poet, novelist, and critic. He was born in County Waterford and attended University College Cork, where he was part of a resurgence of literary activity under the inspiration of John Montague. He has published seven collections of poetry, including *The Sorrow Garden, The Lost Province, Mr. Dineen's Careful Parade, The Last Geraldine Officer,* and *Merchant Prince*.

BILL MCKIBBEN is an author, environmentalist, and founder of 350.org, the first planet-wide, grassroots climate change movement. His books include *The End of Nature, Eaarth: Making a Life on a Tough New Planet,* and *Oil and Honey: The Education of an Unlikely Activist*.

PAULA MEEHAN, poet and playwright, lives in her native Dublin. She has published six collections of poetry, most recently *Painting Rain*. She is Ireland Professor of Poetry for 2013 to 2016.

ROBERT MORGAN teaches at Cornell University. He has written nineteen books of poetry.

LISEL MUELLER was born in Hamburg, Germany, and immigrated to America at age fifteen. She is the author of ten books of poetry. *Alive Together: New and Selected Poems* won the Pulitzer Prize in 1997. In 2002 she won the Ruth Lily Poetry Prize.

AMY NASH is communications manager for Meyer, Scherer & Rockcastle, a Minneapolis architecture firm. She has completed a poetry collection, *Caryatid,* and writes *Night & Day Poems of Amy Nash,* an original poetry blog (http://arambler.com).

PABLO NERUDA (1904–1973) was a Chilean poet and ambassador. He won the Nobel Prize for Literature in 1971.

AIMEE NEZHUKUMATATHIL has written several award-winning poetry collections. She has received a Pushcart Prize and an NEA fellowship and is professor of English at the State University of New York–Fredonia.

JOAN NICHOLSON began her writing journey in 1960, when she took the bus from Los Angeles to New York City after college. Gradually she transformed journal entries into poems. Her collection *My Coat Is a House* was published in 2008.

NAOMI SHIHAB NYE is the author of ten volumes of poems, including *Honeybee: Poems and Short Prose.* She is also a songwriter and novelist. Born to a Palestinian father and American mother, she regards herself a "wandering poet" but calls San Antonio home.

MARY OLIVER is a Pulitzer Prize–winning poet and author of many collections, including *American Primitive,* from which the poems in this book are reprinted. She wrote two books on poetics, *A Poetry Handbook* and *Rules of the Dance.*

JOE PADDOCK has written several books of poetry, including *A Sort of Honey* and *Circle of Stones,* as well as a biography of the environmentalist Ernest Oberholtzer, *Keeper of the Wild*. He lives in Litchfield, Minnesota.

LINDA PASTAN is a former poet laureate of Maryland. Her many books include *Carnival Evening: New and Selected Poems, 1968–1998* and *Queen of a Rainy Country*.

SYLVIA PLATH (1932–1963) was a gifted poet often associated with the Confessional movement. Only one collection, *Colossus*, was published prior to her suicide, but her husband, Ted Hughes, published four volumes of her work posthumously, including *Ariel* and *The Collected Poems*, which was awarded the Pulitzer Prize in 1982.

LIA PURPURA has published three collections of poems, *King Baby*, *Stone Sky Lifting*, and *The Brighter the Veil*; three collections of essays, *Rough Likeness*, *On Looking*, and *Increase*; and one collection of translations, *Poems of Grzegorz Musiał: Berliner Tagebuch and Taste of Ash*. Her poem "Bee" was awarded the Randall Jarrell Prize.

JERI REILLY, a Minnesota native, writes poems, essays, and short fiction. Her work has been published in anthologies in the United States and Ireland, and her poem "Valentines" was selected in 2010 to be stamped into the sidewalks of St. Paul, Minnesota. She spends her summers writing in Ireland deep in the bee-loud glade.

JAMES SILAS ROGERS has degrees in Irish studies, public relations management, and English. He has written on regional Irish history for *New Letters*, *Minnesota's Irish*, *Elysian Fields Quarterly*, *The Encyclopedia of the Irish in America*, and *New Perspectives on the Irish Diaspora*.

PATTIANN ROGERS is the author of ten books of poetry and a book of essays, *The Grand Array*. *Firekeeper: New and Selected Poems* was a finalist for the Lenore Marshall Poetry Prize, and *Song of the New World Becoming* was a finalist for the Los Angeles Times Book Prize. She lives in Colorado.

PAUL B. ROTH is editor and publisher of the journal *The Bitter Oleander: A Journal of Contemporary International Poetry and Short Fiction* and publishes poetry books through Bitter Oleander Press. He lives in upstate New York.

RUMI (1207–1273), also known as Jalāl ad-Dīn Muhammad Balkhī, Jalāl ad-Dīn Muhammad Rūmī, Mevlana or Mawlānā, Mevlevi or Mawlawī, was a Persian poet, jurist, theologian, and Sufi mystic. The translations of his poems by Coleman Barks have been widely read.

JAY SALTER is a poet, piper, and environmental sound recordist who lives north of Santa Cruz on the California coast in a cabin by a creek. He has written several chapbooks of poetry and teaches poetry in outdoor settings. He records environmental sounds for museums and visitor centers. His website is www .aldersong.com.

ROBERT SAMAROTTO (1933–2003) was a poet and a musician in the New Music group Zeitgeist. He lived in River Falls, Wisconsin.

FIONA SAMPSON grew up on the west coast of Wales and in Gloucestershire. She was educated at the Royal Academy of Music and, after a brief career as a concert violinist, at Oxford University, where she won the Newdigate Prize. Author of twenty books, she lives in Coleshill, Oxfordshire.

WILLIAM SHAKESPEARE (1564–1616), often called England's national poet, is regarded as the most widely read dramatist in the world. Ranging from tragedy to comedy, his plays and poems remain popular.

JO SHAPCOTT wrote "I Tell the Bees" as the first in a series of six poems for the City of London Festival in 2010. She used talismans such as a bee pencil to inspire her when writing the poems.

SU SMALLEN is the author of three collections of poetry: *Buddha, Proof,* a Minnesota Book Award finalist; *Weight of Light,* nominated for the Pushcart Press Editor's Book Award; and *Wild Hush*. She was a founding member of the Laurel Poetry Collective, which published books and broadsides for ten years. Formerly a professional choreographer and dancer, she and her poetry were featured in the documentary dance film *Klatch*. Her website is www.susmallen.com.

THOMAS R. SMITH is a poet and teacher in River Falls, Wisconsin. His seven books of poems include *The Foot of the Rainbow* and *The Glory*. He has edited several books, most recently *Airmail: The Letters of Robert Bly and Tomas Tranströmer*. He posts essays and poems at www.thomasrsmithpoet.com.

MARLA SPIVAK is an entomologist and Distinguished McKnight University Professor at the University of Minnesota. In 2010 she was awarded a grant from the MacArthur Foundation for her pioneering research on honeybees. She heads the university's Bee Lab (www.beelab.umn.edu).

KIM STAFFORD teaches at Lewis and Clark College in Portland, Oregon. His books include *Early Morning* (a memoir of his father, the poet William Stafford) and *A Thousand Friends of Rain: New and Selected Poems*.

WILLIAM STAFFORD (1914–1993) was a poet and pacifist from Lake Oswego, Oregon. He published many books of poetry and prose. In 1970 he was named Consultant in Poetry to the Library of Congress, and in 1975 he was made poet laureate of Oregon. Many of his poems are collected in *The Way It Is: New and Selected Poems*.

PAULINE STAINER is an English poet living in Hadleigh, Suffolk. Her neoromantic poetry explores sacred myth, legend, history in landscape, human feeling, and their connections to the "inner landscapes" of the imaginative mind.

ANNE STEVENSON was born in Cambridge, England, and educated in the United States. Her many poetry collections include

Poems 1955–2005, which won her the Neglected Masters Award from the Poetry Society of America in 2007 and a Lifetime Achievement Award from the Lannan Foundation. Recent collections include *Stone Milk, Astonishment,* and *The Thousand-Year Minutes,* translations of the Russian poems of Eugene Dubnov.

JOYCE SUTPHEN, poet laureate of Minnesota, grew up on a family farm near St. Joseph, Minnesota, and teaches at Gustavus Adolphus College in St. Peter, Minnesota. Her award-winning books include *Coming Back to the Body* and *Renaming the Stars.* Her most recent volume is *First Words.*

BARTON SUTTER has won the Minnesota Book Award in three different categories: poetry, fiction, and creative nonfiction. He grew up next door to John Wetzler, about whom Sylvia A. Johnson wrote the children's book *A Beekeeper's Year.* He now lives in Duluth, where he and his wife keep a garden and small orchard, assisted, naturally, by bees.

MAY SWENSON (1913–1989) is one of the most important and original poets of the twentieth century, as hailed by the noted critic Harold Bloom. Much of her later poetry, such as the collection *Iconographs,* was devoted to children. She translated the work of contemporary Swedish poets, including Nobel Laureate Tomas Tranströmer.

MARY SZYBIST is the author, most recently, of *Incarnadine,* winner of the 2013 National Book Award for Poetry. A native of Williamsport, Pennsylvania, she now lives in Portland, Oregon, where she teaches at Lewis and Clark College.

ALFRED LORD TENNYSON (1809–1892) was poet laureate of England for much of Queen Victoria's reign and has remained one of England's most popular poets.

MAURICE THOMPSON (1844–1901) wrote on topics ranging from local history to archery. His first book, *Hoosier Mosaics,* published in 1875, was a collection of short stories illustrating the people and atmosphere of small Indiana towns. He published several collections of naturalistic poems, which were not well received during his time.

JEANIE TOMASKO received the Lorine Niedecker Poetry Award from the Council for Wisconsin Writers in 2014. *The Collect of the Day* is forthcoming, and her story/poem "Prologue" won an Editor's Choice Award from Concrete Wolf Chapbook Series. She can be found at www.jeanietomasko.com and in Middleton, Wisconsin, where she hopes to always have a bottomless honey jar and bees in the front yard hyssop.

JEAN VALENTINE is an American poet and was the New York State poet laureate from 2008 to 2010. Her poetry collection *Door in the Mountain: New and Collected Poems, 1965–2003* won the National Book Award for Poetry in 2004.

VIRGIL or **VERGIL** (70 BCE–19 BCE) (Publius Vergilius Maro) was a Roman poet of the Augustan period. He is known for three major works of Latin literature: the *Eclogues,* the *Georgics,* and the epic *Aeneid.*

ELLEN BRYANT VOIGT has published six collections of poetry and a collection of craft essays. Her poetry collection *Shadow of Heaven* was a finalist for the National Book Award, and *Kyrie* was a finalist for the National Book Critics Circle Award. She served as the poet laureate of Vermont for four years, and in 2003 was elected a chancellor of the Academy of American Poets.

G.C. WALDREP teaches at Bucknell University, where he directs the Bucknell Seminar for Younger Poets and edits the journal *West Branch.* He is also editor at large for the *Kenyon Review.* His books of poetry include *Goldbeater's Skin* and *Disclamor.*

MICHAEL WALSH is a poet and short story writer living with his husband in Minneapolis. He grew up on a dairy farm in western Minnesota, where he came out in the local newspaper during his senior year of high school in the early 1990s. *The Dirt*

Riddles, his first full-length collection of poetry, won the inaugural Miller Williams Prize in Poetry from the University of Arkansas Press in 2010.

CONNIE WANEK grew up in Las Cruces, New Mexico, and in 1989 moved with her family to Duluth, Minnesota. She has published three books of poems and was coeditor of *To Sing along the Way,* a historical anthology of Minnesota women poets. Her most recent book of poems is *On Speaking Terms.*

J. P. WHITE has published four books of poems, including *The Salt Hour,* and one novel, *Every Boat Turns South.* He lives in Minneapolis.

WALT WHITMAN (1819–1892) changed the subject matter and ear of world poetry. Revered in his later life as the "great gray poet," and both reviled and celebrated for his unapologetic sexuality, he included all life—including bees—in his great green poem, *Leaves of Grass.*

JOHN GREENLEAF WHITTIER (1807–1892), a Quaker poet and abolitionist, was strongly influenced by Scottish poet Robert Burns. Highly regarded in his lifetime, he is now remembered for his poem "Snow-Bound." He was a founding contributor to *Atlantic Monthly.*

NANCY WILLARD is the author of many books of poetry, most recently *In the Salt Marsh* and *The Sea at Truro.* Also a novelist and essayist, she taught for many years at Vassar College in Poughkeepsie, New York.

MORGAN GRAYCE WILLOW grew up on a small family farm in Iowa. Her poetry collections include *Between* and *Silk.* Her ghazal series was published as a letterpress chapbook, *The Maps Are Words.*

ELEANOR RAND WILNER was editor of the *American Poetry Review* and is advisory editor of *Calyx.* She is on the faculty of the MFA Program for Writers at Warren Wilson College and lives in Philadelphia. Her books of poetry include *The Girl with Bees in Her Hair* and *Tourist in Hell*.

JAMES WRIGHT (1927–1980) wrote many influential and critically acclaimed books of poetry, including *The Branch Will Not Break* and *This Journey*. He published pioneering translations of Georg Trakl and others with his frequent collaborator Robert Bly. His *Collected Poems* won the Pulitzer Prize in 1972.

WILLIAM BUTLER YEATS (1865–1939) was the great poet of Ireland and a prominent figure in twentieth-century literature. About "Meditations in Time of Civil War," Yeats wrote, "In the west of Ireland we call a starling a stare, and during the civil war, one built a nest in a hole in the masonry by my bedroom window."

TIMOTHY YOUNG is the author of several books of poetry, including *Herds of Bears Surround Us* and *To the Palace of Kings*. He has contributed to numerous musical collaborations, including *Snow Has Fallen* with the singer–songwriter Yata. He lives in St. Paul, Minnesota.

Permission Credits

Grateful acknowledgment is made to the following individuals and publishers for permission to reprint poetry in this book. Unless otherwise credited, the poems are published with permission of their respective authors.

"In the Matter of *Human v. Bee*" by Sherman Alexie is reprinted from *Face* by permission of Hanging Loose Press. Copyright 2009 by Sherman Alexie.

"First Light" by John Barr was previously published in *Natural Wonders* (Warwick Press, 1991) and in *The Hundred Fathom Curve: New and Collected Poems* (Red Hen Press, 2011). Reprinted by permission of the author.

"Medicine" and "Ruins" by Karina Borowicz are from *The Bees Are Waiting*. Reprinted by permission of the author.

"Summer at the Orphanage" by Laure-Anne Bosselaar is reprinted by permission of the author.

"Two Native Bees" by John Caddy copyright John Caddy for Morning Earth Healing Images.

"Landing the Bees" by Jared Carter is from *Work, for the Night Is Coming*. Reprinted by permission of the author.

"earth" by Lucille Clifton is from *The Collected Poems of Lucille Clifton, 1965–2010*. Copyright 1972, 1987 by Lucille Clifton. Reprinted with permission of The Permissions Company, Inc., on behalf of BOA Editions, Ltd., www.boaeditions.org.

"Angel of Bees" by Lorna Crozier is excerpted from *The Blue Hour of the Day: Selected Poems* by Lorna Crozier. Copyright 2007 Lorna Crozier. Reprinted by permission of McClelland & Stewart, a division of Penguin Random House Canada Limited, a Penguin Random House Company.

"The Sacrament of the Bees" by Annie Deppe first appeared in *Wren Cantata* (Summer Palace Press, 2009) and is reprinted by permission of the author.

"Bees," "Ariel," and "Virgil's Bees" by Carol Ann Duffy are from *The Bees*. Copyright 2011 Carol Ann Duffy. Reprinted by permission of the author, c/o Rogers, Coleridge & White, Ltd., 20 Powis Mews, London W11 1JN England.

"Bees" by Diane Fahey was first published in *Mayflies in Amber* (HarperCollins, 1992) and is reprinted by permission of the author.

"The Bees" by Bruce MacKinnon appeared in *Poetry* magazine (February 2009) and is reprinted by permission of the author.

"The Necklace" by Osip Mandelstam is reprinted by permission of the translator, Christian Wiman.

"Foraging Honey-Bees" by Thomas McCarthy was originally published in *So Little Time: Words and Images for a World in Climate Crisis* (Green Writers Press, 2014) and is reprinted by permission of the publisher, www.greenwriterspress .com.

"Bees Awater" (1972), "Moving the Bees" (1990), and "Honey" (2000) by Robert Morgan copyright Robert Morgan.

"Life of a Queen" by Lisel Mueller was published in *Alive Together: New and Selected Poems* (Louisiana State University Press, 1996) and is reprinted by permission of the author and publisher.

"Not Just a Question of Fertility" by Amy Nash copyright Amy Nash. Reprinted by permission of the author.

"Honeybee," "Bees Were Better," and "Pollen" by Naomi Shihab Nye copyright 2008 by Naomi Shihab Nye. Reprinted by permission of HarperCollins Publishers.

"Happiness" and "Honey at the Table" by Mary Oliver are from *American Primitive* by Mary Oliver. Copyright 1983 by Mary Oliver. Reprinted by permission of Little Brown and Company.

"A Sort of Honey" by Joe Paddock appeared in *A Sort of Honey* (Red Dragonfly Press, 2007) and is reprinted by permission of the author.

"The Death of the Bee" by Linda Pastan is from *Last Uncle* by Linda Pastan. Copyright 2002 by Linda Pastan. Reprinted by permission of W. W. Norton and Company, Inc.

"The Bee Meeting" and "Stings" by Sylvia Plath are excerpted from the "Bee Sequence" in *Ariel* and are reprinted by permission of Faber & Faber, Ltd.

"Bee" by Lia Purpura appears in *Stone Sky Lifting* (Ohio State University Press, 2000) and was originally published in *Parnassus: Poetry in Review*. Reprinted by permission of the author.

"Service with Benediction" by Pattiann Rogers was published in *Eating Bread and Honey* (Milkweed Editions, 1997) and is reprinted by permission of the author.

"Happy Hour at the Prickly Pear Saloon" by Robert Samarotto copyright the Estate of Robert Samarotto. Reprinted with permission.